Science, Mystical Experience and Religious Belief

a personal view

Don Mason

Emeritus Professor of Cellular Immunology
Oxford University

William Sessions Limited
York, England

ISBN 1 85072 357 5

Printed in 11 point Plantin
from Author's Disk
by Sessions of York
The Ebor Press
York, England

Contents

Note: The four sections above marked ⋆ may be passed over if so desired.

The Author

DON MASON obtained his honours degree in Physics at University College, London in 1958 and worked for the next ten years for the UK Atomic Energy Authority, first at Harwell and then at the Culham Laboratory near Abingdon. The aim of this research was to release energy from the fusion of isotopes of hydrogen in a controlled and productive way rather than explosively as in the H bomb. Having concluded that there were few prospects of obtaining useful quantities of electricity from the fusion of light nuclei within his working lifetime he changed career and obtained his medical degree from Oxford University in 1973. For the following 26 years, until his retirement aged 65, he carried out research on the immune system at the Sir William Dunn School of Pathology, Oxford. For the last 8 years of that period he was the director of the Medical Research Council Cellular Immunology Unit and Professor of Cellular Immunology.

Contact details:
Don Mason
Emeritus Professor of the University of Oxford
Home address: 5 Larch Lane, Witney, Oxfordshire. OX28 1AG
Telephone:01993 702518
email: donmahalla@donmason41961.wanadoo.co.uk

Preface

SCIENCE, DESPITE its impressive progress in discovering the natural laws that govern the material world, can give no explanation of why these laws have the form that they do. However, by extending the range of the human senses by the development of microscopes and telescopes, science has revealed a universe that is even more awe-inspiring in its scale, complexity and beauty than our unaided vision had shown us. Further, the fruitful collaboration between experimental and theoretical physics has forced a realisation that what we regard as 'common sense' about the physical world is no more than what we have learned to regard as normal as a consequence of our experiences in childhood. For some such 'common sense' is the ultimate criterion of what is possible and what is not; yet, even our own consciousness, the instrument of our awareness, is a profound mystery and the fact that all life ends in bodily death raises in our minds the imperative perennial question of whether such death is the end of our existence.

A mass of data, including much that has been accrued by systematic laboratory experiments, has amply confirmed the existence of those paranormal phenomena that lend themselves to laboratory investigation: telepathy, seeing-at-distance, and precognition. Some of these findings are described in this book and in the references therein. In addition the existence of spontaneous paranormal events, such as Near-Death-Experiences and the apparent recollection of past lives by children raises the possibility that the full range of paranormal phenomena is larger than laboratory experiments alone can indicate. Despite our unwillingness to discard a purely physical model of reality the weight of the evidence is such that we now have to accept that the view that our five senses give us of the universe is wholly inadequate. For many such a paradigm shift is vigorously rejected but such rejection does not in any way diminish the need to make it.

A combination of what science shows us and what studies of the paranormal reveal gives us some of the foundations on which to build a view of the world and our place in it. This view must contain our humanity, our sense of beauty, our artistic creativity and our love. Inevitably, we do not get final answers to those questions that are most vital to us but we do get glimpses and these uplift us and give meaning to our lives. This book is an account of what my life has led me to believe regarding these questions. Any answers must of necessity be incomplete but I do believe we have an eternity before us and, even those questions that we are at present too ignorant to ask will ultimately become open to us.

Don Mason
Emeritus Professor University of Oxford

for Mahalla

PART I

The scope and limitations of science

Introduction

The symbolic nature of the entities of physics is generally recognised; and the scheme of physics is now formulated in such a way as to make it almost self-evident that it is a partial aspect of something wider......The problem of the scientific world is part of a broader problem – the problem of all experience......We know that there are regions of the human spirit untrammelled by the world of physics. In the mystic sense of the creation around us, in the expression of art, in a yearning towards God, the soul grows upward and finds fulfilment of something implanted in its nature... Whether in the intellectual pursuits of science or in the mystical pursuit of the spirit, the light beckons ahead and the purpose surging in our nature responds.

Sir Arthur Eddington (1)

THIS BOOK IS written with the realisation that having passed the age of 70 years, now may be an appropriate time for me to put my own thoughts in order. Of my four siblings, three are dead, two before the age of sixty and one aged seventy-three. In addition, my first-born son died of leukaemia in early childhood. Events similar to these, which we all experience at some time in our lives, inevitably provoke deep questions in all but the least curious of us. This book contains what I feel that my own life has taught me about them. Of course, my own death is yet to come and what is the most interesting (and controversial) question of all must await that event.

Scientific enquiry is based on the assumption that natural phenomena are governed by physical and chemical laws, which are

1

commonly regarded as immutable. Evidence for the validity of this assumption is not difficult to find and the corpus of scientific knowledge bears ample witness to that fact. In contrast, human experience as it relates to our personal lives can give the appearance of being arbitrary, with fortune, or misfortune playing a major part. If this appearance of arbitrariness is real, then one may argue that human life is of no enduring significance, being no more than the accumulated outcome of a series of chance events. However, this view seems inconsistent with the existence of a Universe that displays such order and beauty and that induces in us a profound sense of awe. We are moved by the song of a skylark, the first smile of a young baby and the galaxy of stars visible on a cloudless night. In short, we want human life, with all its vagaries, to be intelligible and subject to some law, however difficult it may be to define what that law should be. Of course, most of the major world religions affirm that such a law exists 'it is the will of God'. Currently Western culture is in a very materialistic phase, which excludes from existence anything that has no objective reality, i.e. that is not manifest, either directly or indirectly via the tools of scientific enquiry, to at least one of man's five senses. In contrast, religion embraces all phenomena, whether material or spiritual, as manifestations of some creative power.

The success of science in accounting for natural phenomena has been taken by some to imply that all human experience is ultimately a manifestation of the forces of nature that dictate the interactions between the constituent particles of the physical world. Of course, there are some scientists and philosophers who maintain that the material world is all there is so, perforce, the world and all that is in it, including ourselves, must be reducible to physical, chemical and biochemical processes. If this were the case the remaining challenge to the scientist would be to define precisely just what are these processes but the challenge to mankind would be to find any lasting purpose in life.

The weight that the materialist gives to sensory experience invites enquiry into just how reliable is the evidence of the senses and whether information might sometimes be acquired by extrasensory means. One recognises that, in as much that the evidences of our senses plays such a vital role in our biological survival we can affirm that in this role at least we can place credence in what our senses tell us. However, despite the fact that every-day experience confirms that our senses can be relied upon to give us a dependable and useful view of the physical world, this success cannot logically be used as evidence against the belief that information can sometimes also be acquired other than through the senses. Further, as has been frequently demonstrated, hypnosis can readily be used to produce major distortions in perception mediated by the five senses (2a, 3a) so that even where the materialistic view seems so well founded, there are difficulties with the belief that sensory input is invariably reliable. Later in this writing I shall give my own reasons for rejecting the materialistic view of reality but before doing so I shall consider just what science can do and what are its limitations. I shall limit my discussion to the physical sciences, principally because the issues to consider are, perhaps, most readily identified in the quantitative investigations of natural phenomena and because, of all the sciences, physics is the most advanced.

The Scientific Approach to the Study of Natural Phenomena

Since man developed the capacity for abstract thought he has sought explanations for what he perceived in the world around him. The search for such explanations was no doubt driven, in part at least, by fear of natural phenomena such as thunderstorms, earthquakes, floods and droughts. As the origins of these phenomena were a complete mystery, early man often attributed them to the activities of Gods. Pantheism was prevalent in the civilisations of Greece and Rome and it was not uncommon, for example, for Roman legions to add to their pantheon the local Gods of the areas that they conquered. We may contrast this past view of the causes of natural events with the one generally accepted today. There is no place for artistic interpretation, religious dogma or political edicts in the study of science. This characteristic of science is its strength and those who have challenged science in its proper sphere of activity, have failed. Two historically important examples come to mind: the insistence by the Catholic church of the 16th century, on theological grounds, for the geocentric model of the solar system and the more recent challenge to modern genetics by the Communist Party in the Soviet Union; the Lysenko controversy. In both cases the powers of the time persecuted the scientific 'heretics' but to no avail.

If science is so successful in providing explanations of natural events it is necessary to ask what we mean by the word 'explain'. In my view its meaning is limited and to overlook this fact is to ascribe to science a power that it does not rightly have. Before I attempt to say why I hold this view it is useful to consider how scientific knowledge, as commonly accepted, has developed.

It seems to be one of the fundamental features of nature that fundamental physical laws are described in terms of a mathematical theory of great beauty and power, needing quite a high standard of mathematics for one to understand it. You may wonder: Why is nature constructed along these lines? One can only answer that our present knowledge seems to show that nature is so constructed. We simply have to accept it. One could perhaps describe the situation by saying that God is a mathematician of a very high order, and He used very advanced mathematics in constructing the Universe. Paul Dirac (4)

The initial stimulus for quantitative measurement, an essential prerequisite for the formulation of scientific theory in the physical sciences, appears to be related to trade, surveying and agriculture (5a). Thus in Babylon from about 4500 BC onwards, units of length and weight were defined as essential adjuncts to trade and some of the elements of geometry were established as a solution to problems associated with land surveying. Similarly, the needs of agriculture to predict the seasons of the year provided a stimulus to the study of astronomy and the Babylonian astronomers developed their science to the point where they could predict eclipses. However, these early studies of the world were interwoven with magical concepts so that the advances in astronomy were accompanied by the development of a sophisticated system of astrology.

As Greek civilisation began to flourish the magical interpretation of natural phenomena began to be challenged. For example, in the 6th century BC Pythagoras recognised mathematical relationships in musical scales and believed that many natural phenomena could be described mathematically (how right he was). Nonetheless, it was many centuries before science escaped the bonds imposed upon it, both by religious dogma and by superstition. To illustrate this point I shall take a specific example, that of the explanation of the motion of the planets around the sun. I have made this choice because it was the first topic that lead to a major clash between science and religion and second, because it is one where a mechanistic explanation of planetary orbits has been totally successful.

From antiquity it was seen that the sun, moon and stars rose in the East and set in the West; the most obvious interpretation being that the heavenly bodies rotated round the earth once each day. Aristotle 384-322 BC was a proponent of this view. He maintained that the earth was the centre of the Universe and was stationary. He also taught that everything beneath the orbit of the moon was composed of the four elements earth, air, fire and water and everything above it by aether. Aristotle's influence was immense and extended into the Middle Ages when he was simply referred to as 'The Philosopher'.

Within 100 years of the death of Aristotle his geocentric cosmology was challenged by Aristarchus of Samos c. 310-230 BC. He was an Alexandrian astronomer who proved by direct observation that the sun was much further away from the earth than the moon and he maintained that the sun was the centre of the planetary system. However, presumably because of the esteem with which Aristotle was held, this view remained essentially neglected until the 15th century AD.

In contrast to these conflicting speculations, Eratosthenes c 276-184 BC also a Greek astronomer at Alexandria, proved that the world was round and measured its circumference to an accuracy (rather fortuitously perhaps) of 50 miles. He also estimated the distance between the earth and the sun as 90 million miles; a figure that is only 3% too low. While these observations had no direct bearing on the issue of whether the geocentric or heliocentric view of the solar system was correct, they were an early demonstration of the scientific method, where detailed observation precedes theory.

An early difficulty with the Aristotelian view of the solar system, that arose from direct observation, originated with Hipparchus c 190-125 BC who has been called the greatest astronomical observer of antiquity. He measured the length of the solar year to an accuracy of seven minutes but, more importantly, drew attention to the planets (Gk. planetos, wanderers). The movements of the planets relative to the 'fixed' stars showed their orbits could not be perfect circles.

This conclusion was contrary to the earlier view which held that, because the circle had perfect symmetry, the heavenly bodies should all have circular orbits as manifestations of the perfection of nature. To account for the irregular motions of the planets while retaining the geocentric view of the solar system Ptolemy (c.100-168 AD), a Greek astronomer who worked at Alexandria, adopted the concept of epicycles that had first been proposed by Hipparchus some 300 years earlier. Planets revolved around the earth in orbits that were essentially circular but with smaller circles superimposed. To fit the data most accurately the earth was not exactly in the centre of the orbits of the planets. The scheme, although complex, retained the perfect circle (+epicycles) and fitted observations very well (though not perfectly).

The collapse of the Ptolemaic system took a long time, over 1300 years. (Although recall that Aristarchus of Samos had proposed the heliocentric Universe 300 years before Ptolemy). Several individuals played a part in overturning the geocentric model and again detailed quantitative measurement was the key (scientists are sometimes accused of measuring everything. It is a criticism that gives satisfaction to the scientist!). The first challenge, in the Christian era, to Ptolemy's geocentric Universe was made in 1543 AD by a Catholic priest, Nicholas Copernicus. He put the sun at the centre of the Universe in his book De Revolutionibus Orbium Coelestium (on the revolution of the celestial spheres). Although a more simple system than Ptolemy's the heliocentric model still did not fit the observations perfectly.

To properly establish the validity of the heliocentric view of the solar system required the application of the power of the scientific method. First, detailed observation, then the search for some unifying concepts which allow the formulation of an appropriate theory and then, ideally, the demonstration that the new theory makes testable predictions that can be used either to support or refute the theory. The detailed observations were made by Tycho Brahe 1546-1601, who was born in Sweden. He made very precise measurements of the positions of stars and planets over many years. Paradoxically, he rejected the Copernican heliocentric model, possibly because the predictions of the model did not accord precisely with his own observations.

The next step in the overthrow of the heliocentric system was taken by Johannes Kepler 1571-1630 (b Germany). He carried out a detailed mathematical analysis of the observational data of Tycho Brahe while they were both in Prague and concluded that the sun was the centre of the solar system and that the planets revolved around it in *elliptical orbits* with the sun at one focus. The fact that the orbits were elliptical, rather than circular as Copernicus had assumed, accounted for the failure of the Copernican model to fit Tycho Brahe's astronomical observations. Kepler deduced three empirical laws (including the 'elliptical orbit' one) that described the motion of the planets. These conclusions did away with the Greek idea of perfect circles but more importantly, dethroned man from the centre of the Universe. Galileo Galilei 1564-1642 (b. Pisa), who was professor of mathematics at Padua, was at that time teaching his students that the earth was the centre of the Universe. However, his support for the geocentric view of the solar system was about to be replaced by a vigorous and enthusiastic adoption of the heliocentric one. His conversion depended on the use of what was then a completely novel way of studying the planets. Galileo was the first to use the telescope for astronomical observations. Three observations made with it convinced him that the Copernican view was correct. First he saw Jupiter's moons (so there was at least one other heavenly body around which others revolved – an observation that destroyed the view that the earth was unique in this respect). Second he saw that the variation with time of the illumination of Venus by the sun could only be explained if Venus was rotating round the sun. Finally, the apparent movement of sunspots across the solar surface could most readily be accounted for if the earth revolved around the sun.

The next step in providing a scientific explanation of planetary motion was taken by Isaac Newton, born in Lincolnshire in 1642. In 1689 he published the *Principia* in which he proposed (Newton's) three laws of motion that accounted virtually perfectly for Kepler's empirical laws of planetary motion. The difference between Kelper's laws and those of Newton was that, whereas those of Kepler were solely related to the orbits of the planets and were really a very elegant way of summarising a mass of observational data, Newton's laws of motion were apparently universally valid; not only did they account for the observed motions of the planets round the sun, they explained the origin of the tides and remain as applicable to the game of snooker as they are to putting a man on the moon. To formulate these laws required the introduction of more or less well-defined concepts: time, space, mass and gravity. As shall be discussed later, the only slight discrepancy between the planetary motions as observed and as predicted by Newton's laws is the rate of precession of the perihelion of the orbit of the planet Mercury. Not until Einstein formulated his Theory of Relativity was this discrepancy accounted for.

Some Key Developments in Science since Newton

Early man made stone hand axes that remained virtually unchanged for over a million years. Since the Renaissance, and even more so in the last 200 years man's scientific and technological advances have been astounding. The reason for this acceleration in the acquisition of knowledge is not easy to explain, though no doubt the ability to disseminate information rapidly and easily, by means of printing (mid 15th century), made a major contribution. In science the success of Newton's laws of motion in accounting for the orbits of the planets impressively established a fact that Pythagoras had maintained 2000 years earlier, that natural phenomena could be described mathematically.

The success of Newton's theory led, particularly in France, to the growth of a mechanistic view of the world, the Mechanical Philosophy, so that in the 18th century Laplace could suggest that if the positions and velocities of all the particles in the Universe were known at the same instant, it would in principle be possible to reconstruct its past and to predict its whole future development. Compatible with this view was the discovery, in 1846, of the planet Neptune whose existence was predicted by observations of unaccountable perturbations of the orbit of Uranus. It was not until the development of quantum theory in the 20th century that Laplace's view of the predictability of future physical events was shown to be incorrect.

While Laplace's hypothesis was an over-enthusiastic extrapolation of Newton's demonstration that the behaviour of inanimate objects could usefully be described in terms of physical laws over which man had no control, the development of science in the 17th century did have a major social impact; it was probably the most important factor in bringing to an end the torture and burning of witches. It has been estimated that in the 200 years that elapsed after 1484, the year that Pope Innocent VIII gave recognition to the evil powers of witches, over three-quarters of a million inhabitants from Catholic and Protestant areas of Europe were tortured until they confessed and were then burned at the stake.

The view that the physical world was concrete and deterministic survived up to the end of the nineteenth century. In the two hundred years that followed the publication of the Principia this mechanical philosophy established virtually all of classical physics and much of chemistry. These scientific developments demonstrated their practical value and new industries arose in the generation of electrical power and the synthesis of useful chemical compounds. Given these demonstration of the power of the mechanical philosophy scientists were confident enough for more than one to claim that all that there was to discover had already been found and all that remained was to make more refined measurements. This complacency was short lived and the beginning of the 20th century saw the introduction of new concepts that were completely foreign to the mechanistic philosophy that had hitherto looked so secure.

What follows is not intended to give a comprehensive overview of modern physics, a task which I am not qualified to carry out and which is quite outside the scope of this book. Instead, a few examples will be given to illustrate how modern science has demonstrated that the concepts of classical physics sometimes fail to give an adequate account of what we observe. It appears that when we study very small scale phenomena and those on a very large one we have to abandon classical physics and reject the idea that one can appeal to 'common sense' to decide what is possible and what is not. Modern science replaces certainty with probability and paradox, and shows that space and time are interdependent. This new view of the physical world is counterintuitive, if by intuitive we mean that which everyday experience would lead us to suppose. I shall return to this point later.

Complementarity-the wave and particle models of matter

The first challenge to classical physics came from what at first sight seems to be a rather minor problem. When a solid is heated it gives off electromagnetic radiation (radiant heat) of a range of wavelengths. If the solid has a cavity within it then the radiation within this cavity comes into thermal equilibrium with the walls of the cavity that are the source of the thermal radiation. That is to say, the walls of the cavity absorb from it as much radiant energy as they emit into it. The application, by Rayleigh and Jeans, of classical electrodynamics to calculate the emission spectrum of this radiation predicted that the energy emitted should increase continuously at shorter and shorter wavelengths – a result that could not possibly be correct. The prediction of this so-called ultraviolet catastrophe indicated that despite its many successes in describing many other physical phenomena, classical electromagnetism could not account for the emission spectrum of a hot object (6a).

The resolution of the ultraviolet catastrophe came in 1900 when Planck questioned how the classical Rayleigh-Jeans theory required to be modified in order to fit the experimental observations. Using this empirical approach he concluded that the distribution of vibration energy of an oscillator emitting thermal radiation could not be a continuous variable but must occur as integral multiples of its frequency. Thus, if the oscillator had a frequency v, it could exist in energy states $n\,h\,v$ where n is an integer and h is a constant, now known as Planck's constant. On this theory an oscillator would emitted a pulse of energy equal to $h\,v$ when the value of n diminished by one integer. This 'quantization' of energy was a completely new concept not to be found in classical physics and its introduction demanded that the principle of equipartition of energy, whereby the thermal energy in a system is divided equally between its different degrees of freedom, could not be regarded as universally valid.

Einstein took the ideas of Planck even further by showing that the photoelectric effect, whereby light shone on a conductor could cause electrons to be emitted from its surface, could be accounted for if light energy existed in discrete packets, photons of energy $h\,v$, rather than being spread out continuously as classical electromagnetism would maintain. The classical theory of light could not account for the photoelectric effect because the local energy density of light at the metal surface would be insufficient to eject an electron.

The conclusion that whether light appeared to be a wave or a particle depending on which type of experiment was designed to study it led to major conceptual difficulties. To illustrate the difficulty we recall some of the evidence that had established the wave theory of light. Early in the 19th century Thomas Young had shown that when a beam of light of a single wavelength is shone on two narrow parallel slits that are sufficiently close together the image that appears on a screen placed on the far side of the slits is composed of a series of dark and light bands rather than two separate images, one for each of the slits. (Young actually used pinholes instead of slits but the explanation is unchanged). The formation of these bands was readily accounted for if light was a wave. Dark bands would appear on the screen at points where the difference in distance to the screen from the two slits was an integral number of half wavelengths; at such points the waves from the two slits would arrive at the screen out of phase and consequently would destructively interfere with one another. Conversely, bright bands would appear when the difference in path length was an integral number of whole wavelengths as here the waves from the two slits would arrive in phase. On the basis of this interpretation of the band formation it was a simple matter to calculate the wavelength of the light from the dimensions of the apparatus and the observed distances between the dark and light bands. The wavelengths, depending on the colour of the light used, turn out to be very short, of the order of 0.5μ (1μ equals one millionth of a metre).

The next major advance in the wave theory of light, made in the 19th century, came when Maxwell, in a mathematical development of Faraday's observations on electricity and magnetism, demonstrated that light was an electromagnetic wave. By this analysis he showed that the velocity of electromagnetic radiation was equal to the ratio of the electromagnetic unit of charge to the electrostatic unit. Further, this ratio was closely equal to the measured velocity of light. Thus, by the middle of the 19th century light had been established as waves of electromagnetic radiation. The whole system was so internally consistent that Einstein's proposal that light was also particulate, as the observation of the photoelectric effect required, and as Newton had proposed two hundred years earlier, presented a real paradox. If a photon was a discrete packet of energy how could one interpret Young's two slit experiment? Surprisingly, this wave/particle dualism was also shown to apply to particles of matter. In 1924 de Broglie suggested that, just as light may appear particulate as well as wave like, particles might also be describable in these two ways. In 1927 Niels Bohr termed this particle/wave duality 'Complementarity', a concept not found in classical physics. Confirmation that electrons can behave as waves came in 1927 when Davisson in America and Thompson in England showed that electrons reflected from the surface of a crystal behave in essentially the same was as light reflected from an interference grating. Further, by reducing the scale of the apparatus Young's two slit experiment could be repeated for electrons (6b). As the size of an electron is less than 10^{-15} cm there was no possibility that an electron could pass through both apertures. However, both apertures were essential to observe the diffraction pattern of the electrons. By treating the electron as a wave the probability of it arriving at a particular place on the screen is determined by the solution of the wave equation that describes its wave properties. The wave is thus a 'probability' wave. In parallel, electromagnetic waves may be considered 'probability waves' that give the probability of a photon arriving at a particular spot.

The scientific evidence that nature seems to deal in probabilities rather than in certainties is a concept quite alien to classical physics. The 'probability waves' can only give the probability of a particular outcome. The reason that this uncertainty was unrecognised for so long is really a reflection of the small magnitude of Planck's constant, equal to 6.626×10^{-27} erg sec. For example, a 10 watt lamp emits over 10^{19} photons /second and a radio transmitter transmitting 10 kilowatts at 10 Kilo Hertz sends out about 10^{33} photons/second. These numbers are so large that the particulate nature of electromagnetic radiation is completely masked. Another illustration of how the apparent validity of classical physics depends on the smallness of Planck's constant will be given later.

Planck's particularisation of energy into quanta had profound effects on the further development of physics. In 1913 Neils Bohr used Plank's quantum theory to construct a quasi classical model of the hydrogen atom in which an electron orbited the nucleus rather as planets orbit the sun. This model gave good agreement with the observed emission spectrum of hydrogen but failed for more complex atoms. Bohr's theory was founded on undemonstrated (and indemonstrable) assumptions about the physics of electrons within the atom and was thus open to question on theoretical grounds. In 1925 Heisenberg developed a quantum theory of matter that avoided these objections. His theory made no assumptions about the internal structure of the atom but concentrated only on the energy levels within it and what it emitted. Remarkably, Schrödinger just one year later produced an alternative theory, wave mechanics, that was based on the suggestion, already mentioned, that particles might also be describable as waves. In passing we may note that the solutions of Schrödinger's wave equation for the hydrogen atom have considerable aesthetic appeal.

The quantum theory of Heisenberg and the wave mechanics of Schrödinger were shown to be equivalent and both agreed with the experimental determination of the emission spectrum of simple atoms. (For more complex atoms the wave equation becomes too complex to solve precisely and approximate methods have to be used.).

Implications of the Wave Theory of Matter

Uncertainty

The demonstration that particulate matter could be treated as a wave had wider implications than simply accounting for the emission spectra of atoms and molecules. It was shown by Heisenberg that it was not possible to ascribe to a particle both a precise position and a precise momentum. If Δp is the uncertainty in the momentum of the particle and Δx the uncertainty in its position then the product $\Delta p \, \Delta x$ cannot be less than $h/2\pi$ (6c) . This inequality, known as Heisenberg's uncertainty principle, is an innate consequence of the wave theory. That there should be an inequality of this nature can be grasped if one notes that greater the number of wavelengths in a wave packet the more precisely does it determine the wave frequency and thus the momentum of the particle associated with it; but the longer the wave packet the less precisely does it define the position of the particle. Curiously, Einstein did not accept the uncertainty principle, maintaining that 'God did not play dice.' What this controversy does illustrate is just what a fundamental difference there was between classical physics and quantum theory.

It is informative to apply Heisenberg's uncertainty relation to a macroscopic system. For a nitrogen molecule travelling at 3×10^4 cm/sec, with an uncertainty of 1.0% in its velocity the uncertainty in position is only about 4 times the diameter of the nitrogen molecule, too small a distance to be detected experimentally.

Paradox

In 1935 Einstein, Podolsky and Rosen published a paper that is still actively discussed by physicists and has become known as the EPR paradox. It arises as a consequence of the application of quantum mechanics to the situation where a pair of particles are simultaneously generated by the same quantum transition. Quantum theory demands that the two particles are described by the same wave equation irrespective of how far apart the particles subsequently become. The particles are said to be subject to 'quantum entanglement' and the paradox arises because quantum theory predicts that measurement made on one of these particles will depend on measurements made on the other one. This prediction holds even if the particles are so far apart that there is insufficient time between the measurements on the two particles for any information, travelling at the speed of light, to be exchanged between them-a situation that Einstein referred to as 'spooky action at a distance'.(6d).

To illustrate the paradox consider two entangled photons A and B polarised in the same plane and travelling in opposite directions such that each encounters a polarizer in its path. Suppose further that the axes of the two polarizers are at right angles to each other and both are at 45 degrees to the plane of polarisation of the two photons. Classical electromagnetism predicts that each photon has a 50% chance of getting through the polarizer in its path and that the probability of one photon in a pair getting through is independent of the probability that the other one will do so. Consequently, classical physics predicts that there is a 25% chance that both members of the pair will get through their respective polarizers.

Quantum theory predicts a totally different outcome. As pairs of photons are entangled the selection of a particular wave state by one of the polarizers, which allows the incident photon to pass through, selects the same wave state for the other photon. However, as the polarizer that this second photon encounters is at right angles to the first one this photon cannot pass. Thus, contrary to classical physical optics, quantum theory predicts that in no instant will both members of a pair of entangled photons be transmitted through the system.

Since 1935 there have been several experiments with both photons and with particles to determine whether observations are compatible with this prediction of quantum physics. It seems that they are and that we shall probably have to accept the paradox. This conclusion is important in that it illustrates that 'common sense' is not a reliable guide to our interpretation of the world that we observe. The problem has stimulated a great deal of scientific and philosophical speculation: Einstein rejected the conclusion that the observer plays an essential role in bringing about the collapse of a quantum state. He 'could not believe that a mouse could bring about drastic changes in the Universe simply by looking at it'. To which Everett replied that 'it is not so much the system which is affected by an observation as the observer'.(7a) That this statement can be treated seriously by those who try to explore the scientific/philosophical implications of quantum physics illustrates how far modern science has come from the Mechanical Philosophy of the 19th century. It has been said that those who think that they understand quantum physics do not understand it.

In the consideration of these difficulties with quantum physics it is notable that they arise when we explore parts of the physical world that are not directly accessible to our senses. We can argue that the difficulties arise because there is something uniquely obscure about phenomena that occur on a scale that is too small for us to perceive without the application of scientific instruments that allow the detection of macroscopic phenomena which have their origins in the imperceptibly small. On this argument the Mechanical Philosophy, which dealt only with the macroscopic properties of the universe, would appear to be free of these conceptual difficulties. However, this is really a false dichotomy; we should not lose sight of the fact that our awareness of the 'every day' world depends on our being conscious of it and consciousness is at least as profoundly mysterious as quantum physics. I shall return to this discussion again.

The Theory of Relativity

The first decades of the 20th century saw not only the development of quantum physics but also a radical revision of mechanics. Newtonian mechanics, which had proved so successful in analysing the motions of the planets around the sun was superseded in little over 200 years by Einstein's Theory of Relativity (6e). As with other scientific advances, the Special Theory of relativity was developed to explain an observation, specifically that the velocity of light was independent of the motion of the source and the observer. This theory was applicable to frames of reference (observers) that were in uniform motion with respect to one another in Euclidian space. The theory required that the separate concepts of space and time, so familiar in the Mechanical Philosophy, had to be abandoned in favour of a composite one of space-time. The change was fundamental for many reasons, not least because it led to the conclusion that the observed invariance of the velocity of light in space implied an equivalence of energy and mass summarised in the famous equation $E=Mc^2$. This equation provided an explanation of how the stars could emit vast amounts of energy over billions of years. Consistent with earlier scientific advances, man was quick to turn Einstein's prediction to military use and Hiroshima and Nagasaki paid the price.

It is not difficult to show that the independence of the velocity of light on the motion of the observer making the measurement leads to a revision of our ideas of simultaneity. Thus, depending on the circumstances, we cannot unambiguously say, for example, that event A precedes event B. To some observers this may be so, but for others the two events may occur at the same time or even B precede A. This situation is so at variance with what we experience in everyday life that we are reluctant to accept this affront to our common sense. Apparently, Einstein remarked that common sense is the collection of prejudices we acquire before we are eighteen years old. The example given should make us wary of using common sense as an arbiter of what is true.

In 1915,within 10 years of the introduction of the Special Theory Einstein developed the General Theory in which the restraints of uniformity of motion and of Euclidian geometry were not imposed. In this theory gravity appeared as a mass-induced curvature of space-time. The new theory soon received the support of observation: it corrected a minor discrepancy between the observed rate of precession of the perihelion of the planet Mercury and that derived from the application of Newtonian Mechanics. Further, it predicted that starlight passing close to the sun would be deflected by the sun's mass by exactly twice the angle predicted by Newtonian Mechanics. During the total eclipse of 1919 the observations made by Eddington yielded results for the deflection of starlight that agreed within experimental error with those of Einstein.

Einstein's General Theory of Relativity laid the foundations of modern cosmology and has counted among its successes the prediction of the existence of 'black holes'. However, this is not to imply that cosmology has reached a state where all major problems are accounted for. It seems well established that most of the mass of the universe exists in the form of 'dark matter' which has mass but that is otherwise invisible. There is currently no understanding of the nature of this mass. Further, it is generally agreed that the universe is expanding and there is direct experimental evidence that this is so. Such an expansion is formally expressed in the General Theory of Relativity as the cosmological constant, Λ. However, observation also suggests that the rate of expansion may be increasing, consistent with a weak repulsive force termed 'dark energy'. Cosmologists are naturally intrigued by such concepts, not least because they may determine the ultimate fate of the universe: whether it continues to expand indefinitely or reverses its expansion to conclude in a 'big crunch'. Whatever the outcome may be, life on earth, not to say the earth itself, will have long since come to an end.

The Anthropic Principle

It may be thought that science can have nothing to say about such religious and philosophical matters as the relationship between mankind and the universe in which we find ourselves. However, as science discovers the laws of nature it would appear rash, not to say unjustified, to make such an assertion.

> '... is not man an unimportant bit of dust on an unimportant planet in an unimportant galaxy in an unimportant region somewhere in the vastness of space? No!...It is not only that man is adapted to the universe. The universe is adapted to man. Imagine a universe in which one or other of the fundamental dimensionless constants of physics is altered by a few percent one way or the other? Man could never come into being in such a universe. This is the central point of the anthropic principle. According to this principle, a life giving factor lies at the centre of the whole machinery and design of the world.'   John A. Wheeler
> (Center for Theoretical Physics, University of Texas at Austin) in his Foreword to Barrow & Tipler (7)

The above comment, from a distinguished 20th century theoretical physicist, draws attention to the fact that science can do more than make conceptually coherent models of nature, it can provide evidence that the universe was 'designed' to allow life to emerge. The anthropic principle has a long history and the most recent developments in science have only strengthened the evidence for it.

Early developments

In 1802 William Paley, who, almost 40 years earlier had been a Senior Wrangler at Cambridge, published a book, *Natural Philosophy* in which he argued that natural phenomena provide evidence for an intelligent Designer. His book opens with the lines

> *'In crossing a heath, suppose I found a watch upon the ground, and it should be inquired how the watch happened to be in that place…For this reason, and for no other, viz. that, when we come to inspect the watch, we perceive …that its several parts are framed and put together for a purpose.*   cited in 7(b)

He rested much of his case on an analogy between a man-made artefact, namely a watch, and organic structures such as the eye and ear that are found in life. Just as the structure of the watch implied the existence of an intelligent designer, so does the existence of complex biological structures. As we might anticipate philosophers of the ancient world had proposed the same argument in antiquity. The Roman philosopher Cicero wrote in the 1st century BC

> *'When we see some examples of a mechanism, such as a globe or a clock or some other such device, do we doubt that it is the creation of a conscious intelligence? So when we see the movement of the heavenly bodies,…how can we doubt that these too are not only the works of reason but of a reason which is perfect and divine?'*   cited in 7(c)

Philosophy seems to be a contentious subject and certainly not all philosophers accepted the validity of Paley's analogy even in his own day. However, *Natural Philosophy* received a much more substantial blow when, less that 60 years later, Darwin published *The Origin of Species*. It is generally considered that by proposing the Law of Natural Selection Darwin replaced Paley's teleological

18

explanation for the origins of organic structures. In Darwinism variations in hereditable characteristics that occurred randomly are subject to a selection process that has been termed 'the survival of the fittest'. Darwin noted that species generally produce more offspring than their habitat can support. In the consequent competition for survival those genetic variants that are best able to compete are most likely to survive and thereby pass their genetic variations on to the next generation. On this argument evolution depends, not on the activity of an intelligent Designer, but on an environment-driven selection mechanism that acts on each generation in a population displaying randomly generated diversity.

Parenthetically, Huxley, who died in 1895, less than ten years before the demise of the Mechanical Philosophy, made the interesting point that the idea of random generation of variation ran counter to the view that every event was rigidly predetermined by the conditions that gave rise to it. If we take this idea to its logical conclusion we would presumably have to argue that, according to the Mechanical Philosophy all speciation was, in principle, traceable back to some 'initial' condition. It follows that provided one were to accept the proposition that the 'initial condition' was God acting as an intelligent Designer, Darwin's Theory of Evolution would conflict with Paley's argument from Design only if one abandoned the Mechanical Philosophy. Huxley, who supported the Mechanical Philosophy, was an agnostic and we can confidently assume that he would, rather inconsistently, have rejected the proposition.

As has already been described, the 20th century saw the downfall of the Mechanical Philosophy; the physical world was no longer to be considered as deterministic, instead uncertainty and chance were possible. As has been discussed, the limitations on uncertainty are virtually imperceptible in the macroscopic scheme, a feature which accounted for the successes of the Mechanical Philosophy, but at the atomic and subatomic level uncertainty could be of major importance. With regard to Darwin's theory of evolution it lifted the yoke of determinism and thereby removed an obstacle to the refutation of Paley's argument from design as it applied to the organic world.

Although Darwin's theory of evolution was commonly seen to make Paley's argument from design untenable for biological development, Paley also evoked inorganic aspects of the world, in particular the laws of motion and gravitation, to support his idea. He deduced mathematically that for the earth's orbit round the sun to be stable against periodic perturbations, a condition that he very reasonably regarded as a prerequisite for the planet to support life, the gravitational force between massive objects should vary inversely as the square of the distance between them, that the masses of the planets should be small compared to that of the sun, and that planetary orbits should be neither too eccentric nor much inclined to one another. These deductions comply fully with observation and therefore do something to support Paley's case for an intelligent Designer. What Paley did not know was that the 20th century science would provide many more examples of what may regarded as either fortunate coincidences or evidence for intelligent design. By 'fortunate' we mean coincidences that make life on earth possible. No attempt will be made here to present all of these examples but a few will be described. A comprehensive account is given in reference (7).

Developments in the 20th century

By the 20th century chemical analysis had shown that all living organisms are made up predominantly of a few different chemical elements: hydrogen, carbon, nitrogen, and oxygen. Many other elements, such as sodium, potassium, zinc, chromium, iron, sulphur, phosphorus and chlorine are also essential for life but quantitatively they are not so abundant in living organisms as the four commonest ones. The great variety of life forms found in nature are possible only because there is an almost limitless number of ways that these four common elements can combine to make different chemical compounds. The element carbon is unique in this regard. For example, whereas oxygen can react with hydrogen to form only two compounds, water and hydrogen peroxide, carbon can form a vast number of molecules with hydrogen, including ring compounds as well as linear ones. It turns out that there are several fortunate coincidences involved in the synthesis of carbon.

The properties of matter and the course of cosmic evolution are now seen to be intimately related to the structure of the living being and to its activities; they become, therefore, far more important in biology than has previously been suspected. For the whole evolutionary process, both cosmic and organic, is one, and the

20

Carbon is formed in the interior of those stars that are beginning to exhaust their supply of hydrogen that undergoes nuclear fusion to form helium. As the hydrogen to helium conversion slows down in a star it begins to undergo gravitational collapse causing the star to become hotter until the temperature is favourable for the nucleosynthesis of heavier elements. Three helium nuclei fuse to form the common isotope of carbon C^{12}. Because three helium nuclei are involved it was anticipated that the reaction

$$3He^4 \rightarrow C^{12} + 2\gamma$$

would proceed too slowly to yield significant amounts of carbon. However, in 1952 Salpeter suggested that the kinetics of carbon synthesis would be much accelerated if it were a two step process

$$2He^4 \rightarrow Be^8$$

$$Be^8 + He^4 \rightarrow C^{12} + 2\gamma$$

The isotope of beryllium Be^8 is unstable by a reversal of the reaction that formed it. However, its lifetime, 10^{-17} seconds, is of crucial duration; long enough for it to react with He^4 to yield carbon but not so long for this reaction to proceed at a catastrophic rate.

Two years after Salpeter's two step hypothesis Hoyle, whose work has provided much of the understanding of stellar nucleosynthesis, pointed out that the mechanism proposes by Salpeter could only be effective if the carbon nucleus had a 'resonance' at about 7.7 MeV. When the nuclei of Be^8 and He^4 fuse to form carbon 7.37 MeV of energy is produced because the C^{12} nucleus is marginally less massive than the sum of the masses of Be^8 and He^4. This mass difference appears as energy in accordance with Einstein's equation $E = Mc^2$. For the C^{12} fusion product to be stable required that there is an excited state of the C^{12} nucleus to absorb this energy. (An additional, relatively smaller amount of energy has to be absorbed because the Be^8 and He^4 nuclei require enough thermal energy to overcome the Coulomb repulsion arising from their constituent protons). Hoyle's prediction of the nuclear resonance in C^{12} was strikingly confirmed in 1953 where a resonance was found experimentally at an energy of 7.66 MeV.

Hoyle pointed out that nuclear resonance also played a vital part in the synthesis of oxygen which is formed by the reaction

$$C^{12} + He^4 \rightarrow O^{16}$$

Like the nucleosynthesis of all elements with atomic number less than that of iron the generation of oxygen by the above nuclear reaction yields energy; in this case 7.16 MeV. However, unlike the case of the synthesis of carbon, there is no resonance in the oxygen nucleus of the correct level to absorb this energy. As a result of this lack the synthesis of oxygen from carbon and helium is not rapid. Had a resonance of a suitable energy existed all carbon would have been converted to oxygen and therefore would not have been available to play its essential role in living organisms.

Apparently, Hoyle was much impressed by the apparent coincidences that ensure that carbon synthesis was sufficient to allow life to develop in the universe: the ideal lifetime of Be^8, the ideal resonance in the nucleus of C^{12} and the lack of an equivalent resonance in O^{16}. However, since this work of Hoyle a number of other apparent coincidences have been identified by physicists. The study of the physical world and the development of theoretical models of physical phenomena requires the introduction of certain physical constants. The gravitational constant G, which was introduced by Newton in his theory of planetary motion is such an example. Although the General Relativity of Einstein superseded Newtonian Mechanics the gravitational constant G appears in both theories, which is some indication of the essential part that physical constants play in theoretical models of the universe. There are several such constants besides G: the velocity of light, c; Planck's constant h; the masses of the electron m_e and proton m_p; the charge e, on the electron, and the two quantities g_w and f which are constants involved in the analysis of nuclear forces. It is important to note that the values of these constants have been obtained by experimental observation, and are not derivable theoretically from any model of the universe. (Whether further theoretical developments will change this conclusion is an important question, to be considered below). In 1979 Carr and Rees described several coincidences regarding the values of these constants.(8) They conclude

'..several aspects of our Universe – some of which seem to be prerequisities for the evolution of any form of life – depend rather delicately on apparent 'coincidences' among the physical constants'.

22

To illustrate their conclusion we may take two examples from their paper. First, consider the value of f, the strong coupling constant that determines the strength of the nuclear force that binds nucleons in the nucleus of atoms. Carr and Rees noted that if f were only slightly smaller that its actual value nuclei would be unstable and hydrogen would be the only element in the universe. There would therefore be no thermonuclear energy and no stars. Conversely, if f were only a few percent larger there would be no hydrogen because He^2 would be formed by proton-proton binding.

Second, it is evident that the fact that elements synthesised in the interior of stars are found on planets like earth implies the existence of some transport mechanism. When an aging star of sufficient mass becomes unstable it undergoes a supernova explosion. Such an explosion has two vital consequences as far as life on earth is concerned. It results in the synthesis of elements with atomic number greater than that of iron and it drives off the outer parts of the star thereby making its nucleosynthesis products available to new stars and to any planets associated with them. Carr and Rees point out that for supernovae to act in this way requires the appropriate values of several other physical constants. (One consequence of the fact that nucleosynthesis takes place in stars is that our sun, our earth and we ourselves are all products of a supernova explosion that took place over 5 billion years ago-we are made of stardust).

Such fortuitous 'coincidences' in science are not confined to cosmology. The quotation at the head of this section from Henderson, who was professor of biological chemistry at Harvard in the early part of the 20th century, was prompted by his realisation that a large number of substances were uniquely fitted to support life. The chemical and physical properties of water provides probably the best example. (The following list is not comprehensive. For a more complete one see reference (7e)). Water, oxygen dihydride, has a molecular weight that is less than the gases hydrogen sulphide, fluorine, chlorine, or carbon dioxide but unlike these it is a liquid at normal temperatures. In fact its boiling point is higher than any other hydride. Had it been a gas, as its molecular weight suggests it should, there would have been no seas or oceans and no life on earth. Liquid water has several unique properties of its own. Like other liquids it becomes more dense as it is cooled but uniquely when it reaches a temperature of 4°C it begins to expand again. This anomalous behaviour is essential for the existence of aquatic life in sub zero temperatures since it ensures that ice floats on the surface of water where it provides enough thermal insulation to prevent freezing of the water below the ice. It has been shown that ice exists in five different phases depending on the pressure applied to it. Only the phase that exists at atmospheric pressure is less dense than water at its freezing point. Water has several other properties that makes it unique among liquids: it has a higher latent heat of vaporization than any other hydride, thereby making it an efficient coolant in perspiration, it has a higher specific heat than any organic fluid thereby making it an effective stabiliser of environmental temperatures, and it has a very high dielectric constant (about ten time greater than that of glass, for example and higher than any other non-toxic liquid). This latter property enables it to bring about the dissociation of ionic bonds thereby making water a good solvent for most salts.

Discussion of the Anthropic Principle

Had Paley been aware of the findings of 20th century science he would no doubt have concluded that there was overwhelming evidence for intelligent design and probably most of those living at that time would have supported him in this conclusion. However, the problem is complex.

> *...the properties of the material Universe are uniquely suitable for the evolution of living creatures. To be of scientific value any explanation must have predictable consequences. These do not seem to be attainable. If we could know that our own Universe was only one of an indefinite number with varying properties we could perhaps evoke a solution analogous to the principle of Natural Selection, that only in certain Universes, which happen to include ours, are the conditions suitable for the existence of life, and unless these conditions are fulfilled there will be no observers to note the fact. But even if there were any conceivable way of testing the hypothesis we should only have put off the problem of why, in all those Universes, our own should be possible.*
>
> Charles Pantin. cited in 7(f)

It is useful to consider the proposals that have been advanced to explain how it is that the Universe has such properties as to make life possible. Several explanations have been suggested as alternatives to that of intelligent design:

- The 'coincidences' that provide an environment that is able to support life are just chance. No one who has considered this possibility has felt able to support it and I believe that I have given enough examples see why this is so.

- As has been noted, Hoyle was impressed by the apparent coincidences that make possible the synthesis of elements in stars that are essential for life. He did not accept that they were indeed coincidences but as a convinced atheist he rejected the idea of intelligent design. Instead he proposed that the values of the physical constants that were responsible for such coincidences had different values in different parts of the Universe. On this argument life would appear only in those parts that *by chance* has the appropriate values. There is no evidence for such an heterogeneous Universe, but if the Universe were infinite then we see but part of it. Hoyle's proposal is similar in kind to the following one.

- If the Universe has repeatedly passed through successive phases of expansion and contraction starting each time with a 'Big Bang' and finishing with a 'Big Crunch' then, if in each cycle the physical constants were different, one of them might be suitable for the existence of life.

- Finally, in this group of suggestions; if there were an essentially infinite number of universes, all with different values for their physical constants, then conditions to support life must occur in some of them. Only in these universes would there be the possibility of living organisms.

- It may turn out that at some future date it will prove possible to derive a theory that indicates that the values of the physical constants that we find experimentally are indeed the only possible ones that lead to a coherent and self-consistent model of the Universe. A crucial feature of these constants is that, at present at least, their values have to be obtained by experiment. That is, their values are not predicted by the theories that introduce them. In this sense all theories in physics may be regarded as incomplete and empirical. In 1923 Eddington attempted by logical reasoning alone to deduce what the values of the physical constants must be. This objective has been termed 'the philosopher's dream' by Barrow and Tipler (7). Eddington failed.

Several comments may be made. First, as has been so amply demonstrated, the Universe can be successfully described in terms of very advanced mathematics which has required the efforts of the most able mathematicians and theoretical physicists to discover it. However, the origin of the Universe predates the era of these achievements by man by about 12 billion years. To my mind there can be no other conclusion but that intelligent design lies at the core of the Universe. The comment by Paul Dirac made earlier in this book makes the same point. Second, the fact that the properties of matter are finely-tuned to permit life to exist does pose a problem as to how this fine-tuning has come about. The alternatives that have been suggested are listed above but the answer that one favours will depend on one's beliefs; science cannot help here. This latter comment would require amendment if Eddington's philosopher's dream could be realised. One would then be faced with the remarkable 'coincidence' that the only possible Universe was just the one whose properties made life possible. If one rejects this as being a coincidence then it would be very difficult to avoid the conclusion that, right from the Big Bang life on earth was intended to develop some billions of years later.

The Evolution of Life

The status of Paley's argument for intelligent design has changed somewhat since it was seen to be untenable when Darwin introduced his theory of evolution. Short of postulating an infinite inhomogeneous Universe or an infinitely of universes our presence here seems to imply intelligent design as far as the properties of the inorganic world are concerned. Henderson, cognisant of the fact that the properties of the chemical elements and the properties of matter were uniquely suited to the developments of life wrote

'...we were obliged to regard this collation of properties as in some intelligible sense a preparation for the process of planetary evolution...Therefore the properties of the elements must for the present be regarded as possessing a teleological character.'

L J Henderson. cited in 7(g)

Like the great majority of scientist today Henderson accepted Darwin's theory of evolution in which chance plays an crucial role but he seemed forced to conclude that the conditions that were required to *permit evolution to occur* did not arise through chance. The discovery of the genetic code and the determination of the similarities in the genetic make up of similar species has provided overwhelming evidence for Darwin's contention that different species arise by genetic variation from common ancestors. It seems probable that once nature had developed a mechanism by which genetic variation could arise and be tested for fitness there has been a continuous progression of complexity of life forms from the most primitive blue-green algae to man. The most primitive life-forms that are found today are already very complex and it seems that the more primitive organisms that formed the origins of life have left no fossil records. Thus the origin of life on earth, like the origin of the Universe itself, is unknown to us. However, given that our Universe shows evidence of intelligent design it is legitimate to question whether the evolution of life also involved intelligent design at least in its initial stages. There are ardent supporters of both alternatives and the level of the debate has not always been very enlightened. It has been claimed for example, that Intelligent Design is not science because it does not appear in any peer-reviewed literature. Of course this definition of science will ensure that it never will. On the other hand the supporters of Darwin, who believe that chance plays an essential role in evolution, raise the question that if species arose through intelligent design why is it that so many have proved to be evolutionary dead ends?

With an issue like this, which has such significant implications for where man fits into the scheme of things, dogmatic stances on either side of the argument are unwarranted. To adopt either view is an expression of personal belief, and consequently falls outside the realm of science.

Observation as the Key to Scientific Progress – and the Nature of Scientific Explanation

The whole modern conception of the world is founded on the illusion that the so-called laws of nature are the explanations of natural phenomena. Ludwig Wittgenstein. cited in (9)

A recurrent theme in the above account of the evolution of man's ideas about physical phenomena has been the essential role that careful observation has played in the development of those ideas.

The geocentric Universe of Aristotle had to give way to the heliocentric one of Copernicus because of the observations of Galileo. These observations were made possible only by a technological advance, the development of the telescope and its application to astronomy. Further, the careful observations of Tycho Brahe (actually made without the aid of a telescope) enabled Kepler to formulate his empirical laws of planetary motion. These laws provided Newton with the information he required to postulate his three laws of motion, which accounted so well for the motions of the planets. Further observation, this time on the propagation of light, led to a fundamental revision of Newton's laws which Einstein demonstrated were very good approximations for objects moving at velocities small compared with that of light but which failed completely at very high velocity.

Einstein, who was not an experimentalist himself, emphasised that *theory must be preceded by observation.* He was himself acutely reminded of this fact by the demonstration by the American astronomer Edwin Hubble that the Universe was expanding. Hubble's observations forced Einstein to abandon his preconception of a Universe that was timeless and unchanging in favour of one that accorded with the scientific evidence; specifically that it originated in a 'Big Bang' about 12 billion years ago.

Finally, as has been described above, the downfall of the Mechanical Philosophy and the introduction of quantum mechanics was initiated by observations on something as apparently mundane as the emission spectrum of hot objects.

Once it is recognised that the derivation of the laws of nature depend on observation, rather than on a self-sufficient proof of how they must be, it becomes apparent that science does not provide fundamental explanations. Rather, from a mass of observation certain concepts are introduced in the construction of theoretical models of physical phenomena. As described already, those concepts relating to the description of planetary motion were regarded by Newton as time, space, mass and gravity and his theoretical constructs were his laws of motion. These concepts are not necessarily immutable. Einstein showed, for example, that time and space were not separable; one needs the concept of space-time in which measurements of distance and time depend on the relative motion of the observer and the observed. Consequently, there are important differences between Einstein's laws of motion and those of

Newton. It is informative to recognise that Einstein's famous equation expressing the relationship between mass and energy was a logical consequence of the observation that the velocity of light was the same in all non-accelerating frames of reference. The experimental verification of Einstein's equation illustrates how observation can lead to the formulation of a theory that makes verifiable predictions which are not only informative in themselves but that underpin the original theory. With regard to the laws of mechanics such underpinning is not confined to Einstein's analysis. The great majority of observations of planetary motion accord perfectly well with Newtonian mechanics, even to the point where, as we have mentioned above, an apparent discrepancy was used to correctly predict the existence of a hitherto unknown planet. Whether Einstein's theories of relativity will, in due course, require amendment has to remain an open question. Natural phenomena have been occurring for eons of time before man tried to discover the laws that govern them. As long as we do not lose sight of the fact that our formulations may not be perfect, and indeed may sometimes be fundamentally flawed, we can hold to the belief that there are immutable laws of nature, what is not immutable is our description of them. The strength of science is that it is not a system of belief. Theoretical models have to be modified, if not discarded completely, when experimental findings conflict with them and the history of science provides ample examples of the need to abandon erroneous ideas of the physical world. However, such a weeding out process can reasonably be expected to yield theoretical models that are true by all the tests that we can devise for them. It is evident that there are few, if any, branches of science for which we can claim to have reached such a state of certainty.

While, as we have noted, the theoretical models that physics introduces are perforce valid only in as much as they accord with what is observed, they enable us to describe a wide range of phenomena in terms of a limited number of laws and theoretical models and to make predictions of how physical systems described by these laws will respond to particular stimuli. In this sense physics explains natural phenomena. However, if we ask, for example, *why* does a proton attract an electron, the physicist will say that the electron has a negative charge and the proton a positive one and it is a property of unlike charges that they attract one another, that is, it is a 'Law of Nature'. The scientist in question may then go on to say that if electrons and protons did not attract one another we would not be here to ask the question why. To the scientist an observed phenomenon is explained when the laws of nature that control it have been adduced or a self-consistent theory developed that makes testable predictions that stand the tests of time. However, the origin of the laws themselves is questionably in the realm of science. It is immediately apparent that the phrase *'scientific explanation'* has a particular and limited meaning. The view expressed by Wittgenstein with which this section started echoes one by Newton in the 17th century 'Hypotheses non fingo' (I frame no hypotheses) which comment he made with respect to his belief that the concept of gravity enabled one to formulate a theory of planetary motion but that he was not prepared to offer an explanation of gravity itself.

> *Science cannot solve the ultimate mystery of Nature. And it is because in the last analysis we ourselves are part of the mystery we are trying to solve.*   Max Planck (10)

The Pursuit of Scientific Truth as a Human Activity

> *Curiously enough, there are men who lose that feeling of mystery, which is the root of all our delights, when they discover the uniformity of law among the diversity of nature. As if gravitation is not more of a mystery than the fall of an apple, as if the evolution from one scale of being to another is not something which is even more shy of explanation than a succession of creations. The trouble is that we often stop at a law as if it were the final end of our search, and then we find that it does not even begin to emancipate our spirit.*
> Rabindranath Tagore. Sãdhana (11)

The above comment, by a Hindu poet and mystic, is, sadly, broadly true of scientists in the West but it is not universally so. Earlier in this book I have quoted both Dirac and Eddington whose pronouncements have a religious, not to say, a mystical content. Further, even in the era of the Mechanical Philosophy Isaac Newton could write,

> *This most beautiful System of the Sun, Planets and Comets could only proceed from the council and dominion of an intelligent and*

30

powerful Being...God endures forever and is everywhere present, and by existing always and everywhere, he constitutes duration and space.   Isaac Newton (cited in 5e)

The belief expressed in the last two lines of the above quotation may be compared with the Sufi poem, written some seven hundred years earlier, with which this book concludes.

In more recent times one may note that an appreciation of such an abstract quality as beauty has played an important part in the development of science. Abdus Salaam, who, with Steven Weinberg and Sheldon Glashow, was awarded the Nobel Prize in 1979 for developing the theory that unified two fundamental forces of nature; the electromagnetic and weak interactions, said that in seeking a mathematical solution to the problem he was dealing with he looked for one that had symmetry. He argued that as nature was beautiful the solution to his problem should have beauty and this would be assured if it possessed symmetry. Adopting this approach he found the solution that he was looking for.

Salaam's co-prizewinner, Steven Weinberg, also remarked on the sense of beauty he experienced in their work (12).

There is reason to believe that in elementary particle physics we are learning something about the logical structure of the universe... the rules that we have discovered become increasingly coherent and universal...there is simplicity, a beauty, that we are finding in the rules that govern matter that mirrors something that is built into the logic of the universe at a very deep level.

This indication that the pursuit of scientific understanding does not always follow strictly logical lines is very well exemplified by the work of Kekulé in establishing the chemical structure of benzene. By 1865 it was known that a molecule of this substance contained just six carbon atoms and six hydrogen atoms. This composition posed a problem because no structure could be proposed for benzene that complied with the established laws of chemical bonds. Apparently Kekulé had a dream in which he saw a snake swallowing its own tail. The dream provided the solution to the problem of the structure of benzene – its carbon atoms formed a closed loop with the sixth carbon atom being linked to the first. This was the first ring compound to be recognised.

It is notable that some of the greatest scientists have shown a remarkable humility in appraising their own work.

The basis of all scientific work is the conviction that the world is an ordered and comprehensive entity. My religious feeling is a humble amazement at the order revealed in the small patch of reality to which our feeble intelligence is equal.

Albert Einstein (13a)

Our experience justifies us in thinking that in nature could be seen the ideal of mathematical simplicity; but the deeper we search, the more we find that there is to know, and as long as human life exists I believe that it will always be so.

Albert Einstein (13b)

PART II

The broader view

Introduction

AS THE PREVIOUS section describes the revelations of science can have a very spiritual impact on those who seek to discover nature's laws. However, no one would argue that science provides a comprehensive description of what it is to be human. Some may argue that it is only a matter of time before that conclusion becomes invalid but if this is so science will have undergone its own revolution- a revolution that must be immeasurably more profound than that which saw the overthrow of the Mechanical Philosophy. In its literal sense 'science' means 'knowledge' and whether we are fundamentally unknowable one may reasonably question. What we can say with great confidence is that we are but beginners on our attempt to know ourselves.

The Difficulty in Making Generalisations from Specific Observations

There is a difficulty that limits the degree to which we can say that the discovery of the laws of nature unfailingly allows us to decide what physical events are possible. As emphasised in Part I of this book, the scientist's formulation of the laws of nature depend on observation. A physical law is derived as a result of repeated observations of the same phenomenon but the generalisation of its validity cannot be assumed because one can never be certain that the observed phenomenon will *invariably* occur. For example, to maintain that the law of gravity ensures that an unsupported object will *always* fall to the floor, rules out *a priori* the possibility of poltergeist phenomena. While such violations of the law of gravity are undoubtedly rare it is impossible by intellect alone to rule them out (though many scientists do). There is an extensive literature, some from reputable sources, that reports that these phenomena do occur although the conditions that have to be satisfied in order for them to do so are not understood. For a brief review, which includes an account of the scientifically documented Rosenheim case of 1967-68, see Bender, H. (14). As the author, who was himself one of the investigators of this case describes, the phenomena observed were associated with a young woman, Annemarie Sch., who was employed as a secretary at the lawyers' office where the disturbances occurred. Post Office engineers and two physicists, F. Karger and G. Zicha, from the Max-Planck Institute for Plasma Physics in Munich, excluded all known causes, natural or fraudulent, for the recorded malfunction of the telephone system and the fluctuations in the power supply, even when the standard supply was replaced by an independent one. They were equally at a loss to explain why electric lamps became unscrewed or exploded or the hallway lamps began to swing after Annemarie had passed. These oscillations were recorded on film, which, incidentally, excluded the trivial explanation that the secretary had set them in motion by touching them.

Another first-hand account of a poltergeist phenomenon is recorded by Fontana (15). Here again there were many witnesses and some of the phenomena occurred when Fontana, the investigator, was alone in the garage where the events took place.

For a comprehensive review of poltergeist phenomena see Gauld, A., A. D Cornell (16). This book lists 500 poltergeist cases, the earliest being recorded in 530 AD and the most recent in 1975 AD, just 4 years before Gauld and Cornell published their book.

The Problem of Invention

While the scientist develops his theories of the physical world from detailed quantitative observation there are human activities that depends on the development of novel ideas which, while they may rely at the outset on observation, clearly require the ability to conceptualise new structures that have no equivalent in the natural world. To take a specific example; the development of the steam engine required the *de novo* invention of such things as valves, conrods, pistons, cylinders, crankshafts, high-pressure steam boilers, etc. None of these objects are found in nature and the technical terms used to describe them were introduced *after* the ideas about them were conceived. The fact that invention precedes the appropriate language illustrates the self-evident conclusion that, while our thought processes appear to depend on words, it seems rather that our thoughts are translated into words by a process that is quite unconscious. Thus language, while in general playing an essential role in the exchange of ideas between individuals, is not necessary for the thought process itself.

While I have used the invention of the steam engine to illustrate the difficulty that any purely mechanical view of ourselves has in accounting for some activities of the human mind, there are a host of other examples that I might have chosen. In mathematics, in theoretical physics, in music, in poetry and in art we see the capacity of the mind to engage in the highest levels of abstract thought. However, the difficulty of trying to account for human creativity on purely mechanistic grounds is part of a much larger problem that will now be considered.

The Problem of Consciousness

In addition to the difficulties, described above, that science has in providing an understanding of human experience and invention there is another which raises a whole set of new questions and imponderables. Any attempt to produce a comprehensive description of the Universe and our existence in it must involve a consideration of consciousness. As already remarked, scientific laws can be revealed only in response to scientific observation and observation implies consciousness. While consciousness itself may be an appropriate subject for scientific examination, as with the natural sciences we can only hope to formulate a set of concepts and discover a set of laws related to these concepts. However, to what extent even this hope can be realised can be questioned. Professor J S Haldane remarked that

> *If we attempt to describe consciousness as we describe what we interpret as physical and biological phenomena, the attempt is a gross failure.* (13c).

This unique position of consciousness in man's understanding of the Universe and of himself has been repeatedly expressed:

I incline to the idealistic theory that consciousness is fundamental, and that the material universe is derivative from consciousness, not consciousness from the material universe.

Sir James Jeans (13d)

Consciousness cannot be explained in terms of matter and its laws. I regard consciousness as fundamental. I regard matter as derivative from consciousness. We cannot get behind consciousness. Everything we talk about, everything we regard as existing, postulates consciousness.

Max Planck (13e)

Although I think that life may be the result of an accident, I do not think that of consciousness. Consciousness cannot be accounted for in physical terms, for consciousness is fundamental. It cannot be accounted for in terms of anything else.

Erwin Schrödinger (13f)

Although the scientists that I have quoted were writing in the first half of the 20th century the problem of consciousness still remains. The philosopher David Chalmers argues that the problem may be considered as two separate ones; one "easy" the other "hard". He suggests that the "easy" problem may yield to scientific explanation in a century or two but he does not suggest a time scale for the solution of the "hard" one. (17). Chalmers' article contains a critique of recent proposed explanations for consciousness and he points out that none of them explain the "experience" of consciousness, which in his view is the "hard" problem.

I would argue that the problem of consciousness is qualitatively different from the scientific problems with which the physical sciences deal with so effectively. In this sense I am concurring with the views of the eminent scientist whom I have just quoted. However, such opinion on this matter is very much supported by observation. Anyone who examines the *scientific* data relating to human consciousness with an open mind has to conclude that we can, under certain circumstances, acquire information by extra-sensory means. Thus our five senses do not give us a complete and self-contained view of our existence. I am aware that this statement, which is widely unpopular among many scientists, will lead some readers to dismiss this writer as 'unscientific'. However, a survey of the literature will reveal that the writer is in good company. One

36

great virtue of scientific enquiry is that errors ultimately are revealed as such. Consequently one can feel comfortable in the assertion that there must come a time when the purely materialistic image of the Universe will be overturned.

The following quotation, from William James, expresses his view that it is inappropriate for science to formulate beliefs rather than solely to acquire new knowledge.

The sciences of nature know nothing of spiritual presences, and on the whole hold no practical commerce whatever with the idealistic conceptions towards which general philosophy inclines. The scientist, so-called, is, during his scientific hours at least, so materialistic that one may well say that on the whole the influence of science goes against the notion that religion should be recognised at all. (18a)

Not all scientists are as materialistic as James suggests. I have already described the inspiration that some of the most outstanding theoretical physicists have received from their work and the sense of awe engendered by what they have discovered. For some scientists the experience of the numinous is very personal; the French mathematician, scientist and theologian, Blaise Pascal, one of the founders of the mathematics of probability and inventor of a calculating machine and the hydraulic press, had a mystical experience that profoundly changed his life (19a). Contrary to what one may believe, religious or mystical experiences are not uncommon and I shall return to this subject later. Pascal's experience illustrates the essentially personal nature of those events that have the most impact upon us as individuals. Consequently, since the subjects of scientific study, at least in the quantitative sciences, must be reproducible and not idiosyncratic, much of what is most important in human life is excluded from the province of those sciences that deal with material objects. Of course, a materialistic neurophysiologist would probably argue that even Pascal's experience was essentially a consequence of neuronal activity and that a mystical experience will remain such only until the trigger that induced it and the neurones it affects, are identified. I shall return to this issue later.

Currently, the materialistic outlook of western thought discourages the study of those phenomena that appear to challenge materialism. Extensive evidence for this un-objective censorship can be found in many accounts by those investigating the paranormal, and no one, from Presidents of the Royal Society to Nobel prize winners have been spared. As we have seen, the scientific method is most effective at studying those phenomena that impinge on our five senses and on the scientific instruments that have been invented to extend the range of those senses. To western materialism these phenomena constitute the 'real' world and the attraction of this world view is that we can all experience these phenomena for ourselves. Thus, for example, pure water, subject to a pressure of one atmosphere boils at 100°C, regardless of the nationality, race or religious belief of the observer. However, as I have remarked above, there is a range of experiences that are not universal in this way and do not lend themselves so readily to study as those of the 'real' world. When asked, about 60% of randomly chosen individuals will give a positive response to the question 'Have you ever had an experience that you would describe as religious, spiritual, or mystical?' These experiences are personal and usually, though not always, involve just one individual. They can rarely be reproduced at will and consequently, they do not lend themselves to study in the same way as do the physical phenomena of the 'real' world. However, as shall become apparent, they cannot be simply dismissed as an illusion of the observer even if science has its fundamentalists every bit as much as religion does.

Despite the hostility of some scientists to religious belief science has made a vast contribution to our awareness of the Universe and I shall return to this point later in this book.

Human Experiences that Challenge a Materialistic View of Nature

In what follows I shall briefly review some of the observations that have caused me to reject a materialistic view of nature, sometimes termed 'naïve realism,' in favour of one that claims that we can acquire knowledge by means other than through our five senses, that the laws of physics as currently formulated are sometimes violated and that our commonly accepted concept of time is totally inadequate.

People like us who believe in physics, know the distinction between the past, present and future is only a stubbornly persistent illusion.   Albert Einstein. (20a)

38

Initially I shall describe observations made within my own family but will then consider some of the studies of other individuals and groups who have had the curiosity (and courage) to venture outside the province of conventional science.

Hypnosis

I have decided to start this section with an account of my own observations on hypnosis. This subject has attained academic respectability so it is the least controversial of those phenomena that challenge what we naively regard as common sense. All the types of phenomena that I shall describe have already been reported in the extensive literature on this subject. However, in as much as I have been fortunate enough to witness the effects of hypnosis first hand, the subject has formed part of my personal experience and has shown me how little we understand the human mind.

My own father was an accomplished hypnotist who first read about the subject, and then practiced it, while he was still at school. In later years he used hypnosis both to entertain and as a therapeutic tool.

Used wisely hypnosis can be of great value; on one occasion a young army corporal came to my father in an effort to overcome a stammer. This impediment manifested itself only when the NCO was on the parade ground drilling a squad of soldiers. Anyone who has had the experience of marching in a squad will know that orders given by the person in charge must be accurately synchronised with the cadence of the march. A stammer at such a time is consequently a disaster and my father's visitor was suffering covert ridicule by those under his command. My father hypnotised the young NCO and sought the reason for his difficulty in speaking when faced by a group of people. Under hypnosis the soldier revealed that as a small child he had had an accident in class, which had caused his unkind teacher to bring him to the front of the class to be humiliated. Naturally my father had no means of independently verifying this story but while the soldier was still hypnotised he brought him back to the present day and suggested that, instead of being unable to give commands at will he would be unable to move his legs. My father then terminated the hypnotic trance and the soldier left. He returned two weeks later to report that the treatment had been a great success in that his stammer had gone. However, he pointed out that there were times on the parade ground when it was necessary to march alongside the squad he was drilling and his hypnotically–induced lack of mobility at such times was a real problem. My father hypnotised the young man again and suggested that, instead of being unable to move his legs when giving orders he would be unable to unclench his hand. Since hands are clenched during marching this immobilisation was of no consequence. The soldier subsequently reported that all was now well and gradually the inability to move his fingers waned.

On another occasion my father was visited by a policeman whose further promotion was blocked by his inability to do simple arithmetic. In an effort to overcome this problem the man had paid for special tuition from a tutor of mathematics-but to no avail. My father taught the policeman mathematics under hypnosis (hypnotised subjects are not asleep and the term 'hypnosis' is not a good one). Subsequently the young man revisited his tutor who proclaimed that my father had taught the policeman more mathematics in one hour than he had managed in three months! I do not know how many further teaching sessions under hypnosis my father gave but the outcome was that the policeman passed his mathematics examination at the next attempt.

My father's use of hypnosis for entertainment was almost invariably done with the full agreement of those taking part. The sole exception occurred when he was demonstrating hypnotism at an army barracks. The majority of the subjects were army privates and my father had them playing pianos that were apparently visible to them but to no one else. He also had them rolling drunk on nonexistent whiskey. After a few other episodes of this sort a sergeant-major in the audience walked up to the stage and stated in a loud and aggressive voice that my father should not insult the intelligence of the people present by putting on a show that clearly depended on the pre-arranged conscious co-operation of the performers. My father looked the sergeant-major in the face and said 'Look at me.' He then waved his hand in front of the soldier's face and said 'Go to sleep'. The sergeant-major went immediately into a hypnotic trance whereupon my father instructed him to carry out sentry duty in the hall after he was 'woken up'. This post-hypnotic suggestion was obeyed and the sergeant-major spent the remainder of my father's performance marching up and down the auditorium.

Needless to say my father gave all the subjects, including the sergeant-major, the suggestion that at the end of the show they would all feel well and refreshed by an experience of which they had no recollection. (Contrast with my father teaching maths under hypnosis where memory of what was taught was sustained). There was an interesting sequel to this performance. In order to leave the hall where the entertainment had taken place my father had to pass through the bar. There the sergeant-major was being assured by his friends that he had indeed marched back and forth in the hall at my father's bidding. The sergeant-major demanded of my father that he should contradict the statement of his friends. On the contrary, my father confirmed what they had said. At this point the sergeant-major became very angry and called my father a liar. My father asked him quietly whether the tankard on the bar in front of him was his. On receiving confirmation that this was so my father asked the sergeant-major to put his hand on it. 'Now you can't take it off' said my father. And, indeed he could not, much to his consternation.

My father told me afterwards that in normal circumstances he would not have been able to hypnotise the sergeant-major against his will and with just three words. He attributed his success to the fact that the many people in the audience added their own power to his command. In support of this interpretation he told me of an experience that he had when he was much younger. At that time there was an act on the variety stage named 'Resista 'after a young woman of slight build who apparently had the power to prevent anyone lifting her off the ground. Men in the audience were challenged to do so and there was a £100 prize for anyone who was successful. Resista would stand anywhere on the stage that was asked of her so concealed mechanical restraints could not account for the apparent change in her weight. My father recognised that the universal failure of anyone to collect the prize depended on the power of suggestion. He was sure that his knowledge of suggestion would make him immune from it and he went up on the stage fully confident in the belief that the £100 was his. 'Seven stone' Resista's co-performer announced. My father lifted the girl off the stage with ease. 'Ten stone' said the man. My father found the lift required a little more effort. 'Fifteen stone'. My father could barely move the girl. 'Twenty stone'. My father was defeated. In talking to me years afterwards he attributed his defeat to the fact that the audience were mentally on the side of the slim young girl and that they willed all the men to fail.

Other examples of my father's demonstration of the powers of hypnosis come to mind. On one occasion he hypnotised a man of middle age who had been married for some twenty years. While he was in trance my father told him that he would soon introduce him to an attractive woman who would be a complete stranger to him. My father then brought him out of trance and carried out the promised introduction. ' Do you know this lady?' 'No, I do not.' 'Now that you have met her do you feel that she is someone whom you would like to get to know?' 'Yes.' By this time the woman in question, who was the wife of the hypnotised subject, was showing signs of alarm and my father had to assure her that her husband's failure to recognise her was only transient. He then re-hypnotised the subject and gave him the suggestion that he was about to meet his wife and that he would be delighted to see her. To the wife's evident relief this all turned out as my father knew that it would and the pair were happily reunited.

On this same occasion my father gave the suggestion to another hypnotised subject that he was about to be given a beautiful canary. He was asked to hold his finger up horizontally as a perch to receive the bird. My father then mimed the transfer of the 'canary' to the man's finger. The subject, who was clearly delighted with the invisible gift, went round the room showing the bird to his friends. Father then asked him to return to the podium to take part in a further part of the performance. With no prompting from anyone the man took a large glass, laid his finger on the table and then placed the inverted glass over it. He then carefully withdrew his finger leaving the glass up side down on the table. When my father asked him why he had done so the man replied, in all seriousness, that he did not want to lose his canary.

The final example of hypnosis that I shall describe took place in our own home when my younger brother Peter was a teenager. A small group of his friends were present and they asked my father to demonstrate hypnosis. Roger was one of the young men who agreed to take part and my father soon had him hypnotised. While in trance my father gave him the suggestion that at five minutes past eight he would ask Peter to play a tune on the piano. Father then brought him out of trance and the party continued apparently normally with Roger showing no signs that he had been hypnotised. However, at five past eight he turned to Peter and said 'Peter, how about a tune on the piano?' He was completely bemused by the hilarious response to this request from his friends present and when my father asked him why he had made the request to Peter he replied that he just thought it would be a nice idea.

These results of hypnosis illustrate how little we understand of the interaction between human minds. That it is possible, simply through the power of speech, to induce a person to 'see' a canary that is not there illustrates how readily our sensory perception of the world can be interfered with. Indeed, as the existence, or otherwise, of a canary depends on the state of mind of the observer one is forced to ask the question 'what do we mean by state of mind?' It would be of interest to study a situation where two or more individuals, in the same room, are hypnotised to see a canary. Would they see the 'same' canary, that is, one occupying the same location and having the same appearance? If they were in telepathic communication, then the answer might be yes. While this may be no more than unfounded speculation the proven existence of telepathy (see below) does not allow one a priori to rule out the possibility. Further, as the behaviour of the sergeant-major described above illustrates, the actions of an individual can be dominated by the minds of a group of people acting in concert without either the subject, or those influencing him being aware that any mental interaction is taking place.

The fact that my father could completely suppress the memory that a man had for his wife, despite their twenty years of married life may indicate the presence of an innate mechanism whose normal role is to suppress memories that are unpleasant to us. If this is so then such a suppression may be brought at a cost, as would appear to be the case of the soldier who stammered when he was faced with a squad of troops on the parade ground. Conversely, hypnosis seems able to overcome a block in the laying down of memory as with the policeman who could not grasp the elements of arithmetic until my father taught him the subject under hypnosis. Finally, as the example of post-hypnotic suggestion described illustrates, it is possible for someone who is apparently wide awake and ostensibly normal, to carry out a command give under hypnosis without the individual being aware that what he considers to be an act of his own volition is actually in obedience to a command given by another person.

While striking in themselves, these phenomena do not exhaust the possible effects of hypnosis; others have demonstrated that the autonomic nervous system can also be influenced by hypnosis. For example, hypnosis can prevent the release into the bloodstream, of the stress hormone cortisol, which is otherwise induced in a subject whose arm is immersed in ice-cold water. Similarly, a blister can be raised on the skin by the power of suggestion. These effects are particularly unexpected because the autonomic nervous system, as its name implies, is generally considered not to be under conscious control. An exception to this lack of conscious control can occur when the individual under test is given bio-feedback, that is, they can see the effects of their mental efforts to control their autonomic nervous system. One may argue that this phenomenon is an example of the effect of autosuggestion, where the subject acts as his or her own hypnotist.

My observations of the profound effects of suggestion on how an individual may perceive the world and respond to it, especially when a mass of like-minded people are present has made me wary of the power of evangelism, whether of the political or the religious kind. Further, attempts to use hypnosis to enable those in hypnotic trance to recollect previous incarnations is clearly fraught with difficulty. This topic will be considered again in this book when the evidence for reincarnation is discussed.

Paranormal Phenomena

In his excellent introduction to the study of the paranormal Ellison writes:

Psychic research is much more exacting than many other scientific subjects. It forces one to examine the very basis of one's views about consciousness and the Universe. Most of the difficulties met in accepting even well verified phenomena are due to the absence of a complete theory – a model or paradigm – within which they fit. Most 'ordinary' Western science fits the model presented by naïve realism – it is all out there in three dimensional space, and science is the process of examining it (without unduly affecting it). Because most psychic phenomena do not fit this model they are rejected by many so-called scientists: such phenomena are impossible, therefore they cannot happen, therefore they do not happen. (2c)

One might add that a natural corollary of this blind scepticism is that any evidence that supports the existence of the paranormal must be false and the scientific credentials of those who say otherwise are immediately suspect. However, those who have carried out 'ordinary' scientific research will know how resistant science is to the overthrow of an established paradigm. Max Planck once remarked that scientists were generally reluctant to change their long-held views and new ideas became generally adopted only as young scientist became recognised and older one retired from the scene. The same idea has been put more succinctly, if less elegantly as 'science makes progress through funerals'. One should not, therefore, be surprised that the existence of paranormal phenomena, which challenges so completely the materialistic view of the Universe has met with such resistance. I shall return to the subject of scepticism again later in this book.

Telepathy

Of all paranormal phenomena, telepathy most readily lends itself to scientific study and literally thousands of laboratory experiments have been carried out. Fortunately, the scepticism with which the paranormal is viewed by most scientists has had a most beneficial effect in that in no other scientific investigation has there been such a thorough elimination of possible spurious causes for the positive results that have so consistently been obtained. From the data it has been shown by standard statistical means that the probability that the positive results occurred by chance is less than one in one million billion (30b). This is about the chance of winning the National Lottery both on one's first and on one's second attempt.

Those who do not study telepathy professionally may, nevertheless, encounter spontaneous cases of telepathy in their everyday life. Such cases, while acting as the original stimulus for the laboratory investigation of the phenomenon, are clearly not amenable to rigorous statistical analysis. However, as this book is about my own experiences I shall recount the following spontaneous example as it affected my own family and my friends.

My older brother, Jack, was a bomber pilot in WWII and was shot down returning from a raid on Germany in March 1943. He parachuted out of his burning plane (of which more later) and spent the remainder of the war in various prison camps in Germany. When Jack returned home after the war he married Eileen, a nurse he had met in London before his raid on Germany. It was during a visit to Eileen's parents in their upstairs flat in London that the incident that I am about to relate occurred.

Just as the four of them were about to start dinner Jack heard his father call him. The call was so distinct that momentarily Jack thought that father was just outside the window, but he recognised the absurdity of this interpretation when he recalled that they were on the second floor. Jack and Eileen made their excuses to their puzzled hosts and immediately set off for the family home at Chatham. They arrived soon after father had returned from hospital with a 3 cm gash in his forehead. (The hospital had tried to insist that father stay over night in the hospital, as is normal practice with cases with severe head wounds. However, father discharged himself, fortunately with no serious consequences). It transpired that father had been involved in a serious road traffic accident. In his dazed state he thought that Jack was driving the vehicle and he called out his name. It seems that, as near as it was possible to ascertain the time of the crash, Jack heard his father's call just as the crash occurred. I have no record of what Eileen's parents thought of the sudden departure of their daughter and son-in law from their dinner table.

Spontaneous cases of telepathy are not rare and have long since been the subject of intensive study (21). This book by Gurney, E., F. W. H. Myers, and F. Podmore, is a classic in its field and is a compilation of over 700 cases of paranormal occurrences painstakingly researched by the authors, two of whom (Gurney and Myers) were fellows of Trinity College, Cambridge. I have chosen to summarise one of the cases they report (#82) which shows several similarities to the one that I have just reported about my father's road accident. It concerns a Mrs Wirgman, of 121, Dawson Place, Westbourne Park, London. Myers interviewed the lady himself. She recounted that in 1845 she had moved from Germany to a small town in Belgium where she was visited by an English lady who offered to help her find a suitable residence. While talking to her visitor Mrs Wirgman suddenly told her guest that she must leave for London at once. She did not recount the nature of this impulse but left immediately to catch the boat from Antwerp to London. When her cab arrived at her home in Dawson Place she was met by her cousin of whom she at once enquired who it was, 'her father or her mother?'. She found her father dying; his last words, before lapsing into unconsciousness had been 'Fan will be here on Thursday'. Fan was the first name (presumably an abbreviation) of Mrs Wirgman. Her arrival, which her dying father had predicted, understandably caused her relations intense surprise. In conversation with Myers, Mrs Wirgman said that when she left her visitor in Belgium so unexpectedly she undertook the journey to England without any definite notion as to its object.

While this account is very striking in the compulsion that Mrs Wirgman felt to impose upon herself a major disruption of her activities in Belgium, it is not difficult to discover more modest spontaneous cases in conversation with one's acquaintances. In my discussion with friends and relatives I have heard of two such examples. In both cases the 'recipient' of the telepathic message was impressed to depart from their usual routine. The outcome was helpful in both. In one the 'recipient' was an enthusiastic cross-country runner who trained by running eight miles every day. These training runs took him past the house where his mother-in law lived. On just one occasion he deviated from his run to call on her, only to find her lying unconscious on the floor as the result of a stroke. On a conservative estimate the run was made about 2000 times. In the other case a medical student, who normally telephoned her parents regularly each weekend, departed from this routine by telephoning home, again on impulse, in mid-week. She discovered that her father, who had been perfectly well when she had phoned at the previous weekend, had just suffered a heart attack. In this case the odds that she chose to telephone at mid-week just by chance is about 1 in 200.

As a second example of telepathy involving my family I shall describe an event where my mother was the recipient. A few years before WWII my father had learned to fly and he and a friend Roger usually went on Sunday mornings to West Malling aerodrome, which at that time was a civilian airfield with its own flying school. On one particular Sunday my mother was doing some routine domestic chore when she distinctly heard "Roger's not coming, he's got the flu." She told my father. Sure enough Roger did not turn up to go flying that day but in the following week a postcard came from him. It read, "Sorry I could not come on Sunday, I've got the flu." (For younger readers of this account I should point out that we did not have a telephone in the house until long after 1945.).

I shall end this section on telepathy with an account of an experience of my own. Some years ago I was driving through the village of Milton, near Didcot in Oxfordshire. The stretch of road was quite straight and I could see some distance ahead. There were no other vehicles in sight but on my side of the road and propped against the kerb was a bicycle. As I approached a man mounted the bicycle and started to pedal along the road in the direction that I was driving. Suddenly the thought flashed through my mind that the man was going to turn right in front of me although there was no road junction in the vicinity and no one on the opposite pavement. I slowed right down and, after cycling for perhaps twenty yards, the man did turn right. Had I not slowed down an accident would have been unavoidable. As it was the cyclist was quite unaware of how close he had been to being run over. Of course, although the cyclist gave no deliberate indication of his intention, either by giving a hand signal or looking over his shoulder, it is possible that he gave some subliminal cue that I detected. In any event, what might have been a tragedy had no unhappy outcome.

This example, with its inevitable difficulty of interpretation, illustrates the value of carrying out studies of telepathy in the laboratory where such confounding phenomena as subliminal cues can be rigorously excluded and where the power of statistics can be applied to the data. Of course, as my previous accounts illustrate, these considerations do not detract from the possibility that telepathy that occurs spontaneously may play a valuable part in everyday life.

Seeing-at-a-distance

Before recounting some examples of 'seeing-at-a-distance' known personally to me I shall give a very brief introduction of this much-studied subject.

A belief in man's ability to see events that are not directly visible to the viewer predates the development of television by more than 2000 years. All the events recorded in the Bhagavad Gita, part of the epic Indian poem The Mahabharata, are conveyed to the blind king Dhritarashtra by his minister Sanjaya, who has been given the gift of clairvoyance by the sage Vyasa (22a). However, in India a belief in clairvoyance is not confined to Hinduism. In Jainism, for example knowledge is divided up into five different types. In contrast to Western psychology, knowledge acquired through the five senses (Mati) is regarded as indirect knowledge since it involved the sensory organs and the brain whereas Avadhi is knowledge acquired psychically, via clairvoyance or clairaudience. As this does not require the stimulation of the senses by external objects it is regarded as direct or immediate knowledge (23a).

Early belief in clairvoyance was not confined to India in the pre-Christian era. In the 16th century the much–travelled Swiss alchemist and physician Theophrast von Hohenheim, or Paracelsus (1493-1541), wrote:

Man also possesses a power by which he may see his friends and the circumstances by which they are surrounded, although such persons may be a thousand miles away from him at that time. (20c)

Better known for his conviction that one could learn of events by paranormal means, Emanuel Swedenborg (1688-1772), Swedish scientist, philosopher and mystic claimed to have experienced many clairvoyant dreams and the philosopher Kant gave an impressive account of Swedenborg's gift. While staying in Gothenburg, Swedenborg reported one evening that a fire had just broken out in Stockholm. He remained in an agitated state during which time he announced that a house of a friend had been burnt down and that his own was threatened. After two hours he exclaimed "Thank God. The fire is extinguished at the third house from mine." The whole town of Gothenburg was excited by the news of his vision and he was closely questioned by the Governor. Some days later a messenger from Stockholm brought confirmation that all that Swedenborg had said about the fire was correct (24a).

In more modern times interest in the possibility of clairvoyance was aroused, both in England and in France, by the general interest in the paranormal that began towards the end of the 19th century. An account of research at this time, which still remains a classic in its field was given by F.W.H Myers (3b). There have been very extensive experiments carried out since then and have recently been reviewed by Radin (20d). All of these studies produced results that overwhelmingly supported the existence of clairvoyance, or Extra-Sensory-Perception. As with studies on telepathy, sceptical criticism stimulated the refinement of the experimental techniques to the point where no loophole, either real, or theoretical, could be proposed to account for the results. These findings did not silence the most sceptical critics however. It was claimed by one that ESP was an acronym for "Error Some Place." The absence of any scientific substance in this criticism makes it impossible for the researcher to produce an informed reply, but the onus is on the critic to come up with an explanation which is a more specific than "some place". In contrast, it should be noted that since the initial upsurge of interest in the paranormal that started in the late 19th century many distinguished scientists have testified to the existence of the paranormal as evidenced by their own experiments. For a relatively up to date account see "Psychic Research. A guide to its history, principles and practices. In celebration of 100 years of the Society for Psychical Research."(25). From this book one learns that many distinguished scientists, not least Albert Einstein himself, considered evidence for ESP to merit serious consideration. He was apparently persuaded of this view by reading an account by the author Upton Sinclair of experiments that he and his wife had carried out on telepathy in which she tried to reproduce drawing that she herself had not seen. These experiments were published in 1930 in the book, Mental Radio. (26)

As one might anticipate, the possibility that distant information might be acquired by extrasensory means made 'Distant viewing' a major source of study by military intelligence on both sides during the Cold War. The American results are described in detail in Dean Radin's book (20e). As with the studies on telepathy the experimental results exceeded chance by a large margin, as much as a billion billion (10^{18}) to one. In one case the individual being assessed for the ability to see at a distance described a secret US installation with such accuracy and such fine detail that it was initially believed that a breach of security had led to a serious leak of information.

Experiences within my own family

As I shall recount, my mother was a very gifted psychic. I have reason to believe that many of us have a degree of ability of this sort but my mother was exceptionally able in this regard. As it is not without interest in its own right I shall start by giving an account of how my mother's gift came to light.

At Shorts factory at Rochester where my father worked there was a blacksmith called Charles Cook; he and my father became firm friends. Charles had spent several years in India, but not as a blacksmith. Instead he played a major role in the development of the railway system that was being built at the time. The work had gone well and he and his wife expected that India would be their home for the foreseeable future. This expectation proved to be ill founded but how Charles first heard about their early return to England was very strange. The Cooks lived in a house that stood in its own compound and they had several servants. One day the servants came to the Cooks in a high state of excitement saying that a very holy man had come into the compound and Sahib and Memsahib must come to see him. With some curiosity but little expectation they did so. The holy man told the Cooks that they would soon be returning to England and that they would lose all their savings. He then asked Mrs Cook to pull up the sleeve of her dress. As she did so the symbol £500 appeared on her arm, as though tattooed there. One can imagine that the Cooks must have felt stunned at the time but all that the sage had told them became true. The rail authorities in India told Charles that now the technical work was completed they had no further use for him and his post was now the job for a gentleman. On returning to England the Cooks invested all their £500 savings in a business that failed. The accuracy of the holy man's predictions excited the interest of the Cooks in the paranormal and as my father was also interested he and my mother attended a séance at the home of the Cooks. As my parents were returning home afterwards my father expressed his disappointment that nothing had happened at the séance. My mother was astonished by this remark as she had heard many loud noises and could hardly believe that my father had heard nothing. This was apparently the first indication that my mother was a gifted

51

'sensitive'. I do not have a record of the date when this event occurred but it must have been about the mid-nineteen thirties.

The first examples that I shall relate of my mother's ability to see at a distance concerns events that occurred during WWII. As I have already mentioned, my brother Jack spent over two years as a POW in Germany. During this time my mother would occasionally 'see' images related to Jack's imprisonment. She described the appearance of the wire that surrounded Jack's camp. She remarked that several yards inside the main fence was a much smaller one, only about 15 inches (37 cm) high and made of only a single strand of wire. She said that it was no barrier at all; even a child could step over it. Only later did my parents learn from Jack himself that my mother had described the 'warning wire'. Any POW crossing the warning wire was deemed to be attempting an escape and could be shot.

On another occasion she 'saw' Jack walking in the compound of the POW camp with pots and pans tied around his waist. Not surprisingly, my parents could not guess what this was all about but when Jack came home at the end of the war he explained that as a skilled panel-beater he had turned Red Cross tins into cooking vessels and traded these for anything that he could.

It will be apparent that spontaneous cases of this sort do not clearly distinguish 'seeing-at-a-distance' from telepathy as all the images that my mother received were familiar to my brother. Naturally, these observations were not made with the express purpose of establishing 'seeing-at-a-distance'. However, as will become apparent, in the two following examples I shall give telepathy is very unlikely to be involved. (For accounts of experiments where telepathy could be excluded see the reference mentioned at the introduction to this section). In giving these examples I shall first have to digress briefly.

As I mentioned above, my father learned to fly in the nineteen thirties and he obtained his flying licence in July 1938. It was about this time that he decided to build his own small aeroplane. It was designed so that for transport purposes the wings could be folded along the sides of the fuselage. In this way the craft could be towed behind a car. This project created much media interest at the time and I have several documents that illustrate this point. There are letters from British Paramount News, Keystone Press Agency, World Wide Photos, London News Agency Photos, Ltd, and the

Daily Herald all requesting permission to photograph my father's plane on its maiden flight. More informative are the newspaper reports in the News Chronicle of 3rd April 1939 and the Evening Standard of the same date. Both papers carry full articles with photographs of my father and my mother working on the plane. The latter newspaper also has a cartoon by the famous cartoonist 'Low' showing Hitler outside a Polish frontier post. The caption reads. "I'll huff and I'll puff and I'll blow your house down." Curiously there is also a copy, dated simply August 1939, of a newspaper called 'The South Slav Herald'. In a section on page 4, entitled 'A Letter from London', is an article on my father's plane. It reads as follows:

"A PEOPLE'S PLANE

The British motor industry has long been renowned for the smaller or midget types of motor car. It now seems possible that this country is also to be the originator of a midget type of aeroplane.

Mr William Mason, an employee of an important aeronautical works at Rochester, is building a 'plane, measuring only 19 feet (6 metres) in length and with a wing span of 23 feet (7 metres), which he contends will easily be able to be towed from home to aerodrome by car.

It can be assembled for flight in five minutes and in five minutes can be dismantled into a space of eight feet, ready for transport again.

Fitted with a 40-horse-power engine, this tiny aircraft is expected to have a range of 300 miles and a running cost of no more than that of a small car.

If this experiment succeeds, and Mr Mason hopes to have his 'plane ready in a couple of months, the whole field of civil aviation may be revolutionized.

The airplane will be brought within the financial limits of the ordinary citizen and may at last enter into direct competition, as a mode of everyday transport, with the motor car and railway."

My mother's psychic abilities played a not insignificant part in the building of the plane. On one occasion mother asked my father whether a small part of the fuel system had been specially made for him. She said. "It's on the mantle shelf and there is something wrong with it." My father recognised the item to which my mother had referred but he told her that she must be mistaken about its condition as he had inspected it carefully and she was also wrong in saying that it was on the mantelshelf. Instead it was in a box in the corner of the room. To prove the point he looked on the mantle shelf only to find that my mother was right about the location. This discovery undermined my father's confidence in the construction of the item. He examined it again but could still see no evidence of a flaw. Finally he heated it on the gas stove. It fell to pieces. It had been soft-soldered together rather than hard soldered, as it should have been.

On another occasion my mother again pointed out a problem with the construction of the plane. In this case it was due to an error on my father's part. The wings were supported by steel struts that linked them to the fuselage. These struts were made of tubing with an aerodynamic cross-section and the material was expensive. My father had been careful to cut the struts to the required length but my mother, who did not know that my father had cut them that day, told him that he had cut them too short. My father protested that he had not done so and, as was quite true, he was not in a habit of making mistakes like that. Events proved my father wrong. In calculating the lengths of the struts from the plan drawings he had forgotten that the drawing showed only the projection of the struts, not their full length. The ones that he had cut were two inches too short.

These two examples would indicate that more than seeing-at-a-distance was involved. My mother knew virtually nothing about the various techniques of fabricating solid metal objects from separately machined components and she played no part in the preparation of the working drawings of my father's aeroplane. Nevertheless, by some means she was made aware of the defects that my father subsequently identified for himself.

Complex examples

There are clearly cases of the acquisition of information by paranormal means that may involve either telepathy or seeing-at-a-distance or both. One such example is as follows.

Towards the end of WWII my mother was consulted by a middle-aged woman who said very little but who gave her a small brown paper parcel. The use of such an item seems to serve to focus the attention of the psychic on the person most closely associated with the article in question. During the séance that followed my mother said that the brown paper parcel contained a football jersey and that it belonged to a young man who was very keen on sports. She went on to say that the young man had been Christened 'John' but that everyone called him Jack. My mother then said she was experiencing a sensation of flying 'but not in an aeroplane.' This feeling puzzled her but she could give no explanation of it. Finally, she remarked that she felt very cold and she interpreted this to mean that the young man was dead. Happily it transpired that this interpretation was erroneous but that all the facts that my mother gave at the time were correct. Although several of these facts were known to my mother's visitor, who introduced herself after the sitting as Jack's mother, those relating to her son's immediate military deployment were not. These became known to my mother's visitor only after her son returned from the war. The sensation of flying, but not in an aeroplane, arose because the young man was a paratrooper who had taken part on the raid on Arnhem in September 1944. This raid had involved the use of gliders towed behind aeroplanes to transport the paratroopers to the target area. The football jersey was a silk one and it had been wrapped very tightly so as to give no clue as to its nature. Also, as was learned afterwards, the sensation of cold was entirely accurate. At the time Jack was in a ditch, taking cover from the German attack and he was physically cold.

If telepathy were solely the explanation here, then it would have to involve the acquisition of information from both the paratrooper's mother and her son. Alternatively, seeing-at-a-distance could account for my mother learning of the contents of the brown paper parcel but would not account for the sensation of cold that my mother associated with it.

This difficulty of interpretation is, as I have remarked already, not unusual in spontaneous cases of paranormal events. This problem is particularly prominent when one tries to establish whether communication between the living and the dead can occur. Here again I shall defer discussion to later in the article but here follows two examples.

My mother was visited by a woman and her husband who requested a 'sitting'. During this sitting my mother was ostensibly 'controlled' by a person who was clearly very angry with the husband who was berated verbally and almost physically attacked. Indeed the threat of violence was so apparent that my father intervened and was about to bring the séance to a close. However, the visitors reassured my father that all this anger was explicable and they asked him to let the sitting continue. After the sitting the visitors explained that the husband was involved in an affair with a younger woman and was considering leaving his wife in order to live with his mistress. The visitors identified my mother's control as their son who had been killed while still a young man. It seems that the son was very angry with his father for contemplating the desertion of his mother. The outcome was a happy one in that the husband gave up his mistress and thereafter remained faithful to his wife.

While this interpretation may be the correct explanation of my mother's attack on her male visitor one cannot rigorously exclude the possibility that it was the husband's wife who was 'controlling' my mother paranormally. If this were the case then one would have a very strange situation where a mother impersonated her own son and used her own psyche to control my mother and to deceive her husband. To my mind this convoluted explanation of the assault on the husband by my mother seems less likely than that it was the son who was the controlling entity. However, a very striking example of control of my mother by someone who was undoubtedly alive will be given later. It is the only example that I know of to occur in my own family, which fact may imply that this type of phenomenon is particularly rare.

The second example that I shall give of my mother apparently being controlled by a deceased person concerns the several occasions where the controlling person was my paternal grandmother. In life she had never had dentures and when she took control the first thing that happened was that she caused my mother to promptly remove her own. If this most direct interpretation of this manifestation of control is correct it seems that the temporary taking over of a sensitive by a deceased one may involve not only the control of the motor functions of the sensitive but also make available to the deceased the sensory mechanism of the sensitive.

A rare example of communication

It will be anticipated correctly that the uncertainty about the fate of my brother Jack following his failure to return from the raid on Germany was a strong incentive for my mother to attempt to use her paranormal gifts to obtain news about him. Accordingly, on the night of the receipt of the telegram reporting him missing my parents had a séance. They could hardly have anticipated its outcome. There were just the two of them sitting in silence. Suddenly my mother got to her feet, stepped over to my father and grasped his hands in hers. "Dad it's me. "I can see you," said my mother in an excited voice. My father recognised that this was Jack. "So, you've passed over." said my father, expecting that his son was now dead. "No I'm not" was the reply. " I'm all right. They haven't caught me yet." My father then asked for confirmation that it really was Jack who was communicating with him. "I changed my will before I was briefed" then "I must go now. Tell Mum her table is all right." He laughed and that was the end of the link.

My father was doubtful about Jack changing his will as he was keeping it in his own strongbox. However, very shortly after Jack's communication a letter came from the tail gunner of Jack's old crew. (Jack had not flown with his usual crew on the raid on which he was shot down but with a composite one made up from a number of different nationals.). The letter expressed the sympathy of Jack's old crewmember and said how popular Jack had been with his crew. He also said that the last thing that Jack had done before he was briefed for the raid on Germany was to change his will. This document was now in the hands of the Padre on Jack's bomber station. The next day at work my father asked as many people as were willing to guess the last thing that Jack had done before his briefing. Charles Cook made no less than 40 guesses. No one guessed the truth.

To complete this part of my account of this time I shall have to anticipate the outcome. Jack survived, as a prisoner of war in Germany. On his return home my father asked him about the night he had communicated with him via my mother's paranormal abilities. He confirmed that at that time he had not been captured but he had no awareness whatever of the communication that had taken place between my father and himself. One seems forced to conclude that we (can) exist at different levels of consciousness between which communication is, for some events at least, very limited. Paradoxically the level with which we ourselves are not aware can, albeit perhaps rarely, communicate with certain individuals who have the appropriate degree of sensitivity. As I have recounted above, my father and Jack communicated with each other on a further occasion, this time with no intermediary to make the link.

Evidence for survival of bodily death

I shall preface this section by pointing out that none of the accounts that I am about to give are uniquely explicable in terms of communications between those living and those who have died. The reasons for this disclaimer is partly to illustrate how difficult it can be to exclude unconscious telepathy and/or seeing-at-a-distance for the events that I describe. As I have pointed out, both of these latter phenomena are amenable to, and have been confirmed by controlled laboratory experiments. In contrast, it is much more difficult to devise 'experiments' to test for survival. I shall return to this point later but shall first recount the experiences within my own family.

The first concerns my father and a little family history is required by way of introduction. His mother neglected him and his maternal grandmother, disgusted by the way her grandchild was left uncared for, removed him to her own home and raised him as her own. At that time my father's grandfather received a small pension, presumably resulting from his service in the Police and initially he objected to having one more mouth to feed. However, from what my father told me, his grandmother was a very determined woman and she had her way. As it turned out a very strong bond soon developed between my father and his grandfather and the depth of their relationship subsequently played a very important part in my father's life as will now become apparent. By the time my father was eighteen both of his grandparents were dead. My father had no happy recollections of the other members of his family and he was determined not to turn to them for succour. This was a very difficult time for him but a very significant episode gave him the support that he needed. He was walking across London Bridge and he told me that he knew that there was no one in the world who cared whether he lived or died. He then contemplated suicide. Anyone knowing my father would recognise what a strong and

58

resilient character he was and for him to seriously consider jumping off the bridge gives some indication of how desolate he must have felt. It was at this crucial time that he clearly heard the last words his grandfather had spoken to him before he died. "You'll be all right Bill." It was enough to deter him. That evening he returned to the miserable room that was his home and prayed "If my grandfather is a living, sentient being let it be made known to me by raps." At once he heard three loud raps. Determined to exclude coincidence he asked for three more. They did not come. He told me afterwards "You have to be prepared to accept what you are given." This observation seems supported by the experiences of others. Those who demand proof will not receive it. I shall return to this point later.

The remaining accounts that I shall give on the topic of survival concern my mother's psychic gifts.

Ruth

My mother continued to obtain evidence that Jack had survived his last raid on Germany. This evidence took the form of communications with a young girl called Ruth who claimed to have died in the reign of Elizabeth I. For readers familiar with the terminology used by spiritualists, Ruth was one of my mother's 'guides'. Contacts with Ruth took the form of 'control' communications in which my mother's speech organs were used by Ruth to vocalise what she wanted to say. She always used the term "Sire" in addressing my father. It will be recognised that this phenomenon of control was in essence that same as that in which Jack had spoken to my father, with the notable difference that Jack was still alive. Ruth first made contact fairly soon after my father and my mother's crucial visit to the Cooks and she remained in contact even after the war had finished. My parents learned that she had lived at a place called Fulford, near York and she told them that there were now barracks there. My father searched his map of Britain for Fulford but could not find it. However, shortly afterwards reference was made to Fulford on the radio and my father subsequently located it when he obtained a better map of York. Ruth was correct in saying there were barracks at Fulford in my parents' time and I believe that they are still there. My mother told me that Ruth had died of consumption at the age of thirteen. I cannot find this recorded in my mother's notes but I know that many are missing.

My parents' wish for further evidence of Jack's survival was clearly a cause of exasperation to Ruth. "Oh ye of little faith" she said. "If he's not living then I'm dead!" She then relented a little and said that she would see what she could do. It was soon after this that my parents received a communication from the International Red Cross that Jack was alive and had been captured. The information came long before the Red Cross was usually able to confirm that someone recently reported missing was known to be a prisoner of war. Whether Ruth had any part in this, and if so, how we can only speculate.

I shall defer further consideration of 'Ruth' until I have described other paranormal phenomena experienced by my parents.

Brenda Nash

On October 28th 1962 a young schoolgirl, Brenda Nash disappeared from near her home and a nationwide search was initiated to find her. My parents had a sitting on the day of her disappearance and my mother was controlled by someone who was clearly in great distress. (I do not know whether the girl's disappearance was public knowledge at that time.). After my father had calmed her down and reassured her that she had nothing to fear she told them her name was Brenda Nash. My mother then 'saw' where her body lay and the control then came to an end with Brenda no longer as distressed as she had been. A few days later Brenda again controlled my mother; this time she was completely calm and she thanked my father and my mother for the help they had been to her on her previous visit. Six weeks later Brenda's body was found near Yateley in Hants and a photograph of the site was published in the National Press. When my mother saw the picture she was puzzled. "That was not what I saw" she remarked. The following day another photograph was published. My mother recognised this one immediately. It transpired that the first photograph was of the place where one of Brenda's shoes had been found while the second one was actually where the body lay.

Further examples

Not all manifestations of my mother's psychic gifts were as dramatic as those that I have just written about. On one occasion when my mother and father were sitting my mother described an elderly man whom she could 'see' clearly. She described him in some detail, including the gold watch chain at his waistcoat. She used her table to laboriously tap out his name, one tap for 'A', two taps for 'B' etc. She told my father, he says his name is 'The'. My mother tried to find out the word that followed 'The' but just the three letters were repeated. At this stage my father started to laugh though my mother could see no cause for humour. My mother then received a reference from the Bible. 'The Acts of the Apostles Chapter 1 Verse 1'. This verse contains the name 'Theophilus'. My father then explained to my mother that she had accurately described his uncle Theophilus. In his family his name was abbreviated to 'The'.

As a last example I shall relate how my mother's psychic gifts avoided my father missing a visit to the pyramids of Egypt. My father had always wanted to see them and since my mother was not prepared to go to Egypt by air my parents joined a cruise liner in Southampton and sailed there. Just one day was set aside by the tour operator for a visit to Giza and the trip was to be by bus. On the morning of the trip my mother saw her Egyptian guide (whose name was 'Feda' as close as my mother could pronounce the name.). Feda was walking up and down the bedroom in a very agitated manner and this convinced my mother that something was amiss. She went down to the hotel lobby to discover that the bus to the pyramids was to leave the hotel one hour earlier than my parents had been told. My mother rushed upstairs, my father dressed hurriedly and they just caught the bus.

A secondary personality

Throughout the ages there has been the belief that some entity, usually described as a demon or the devil, depending on the cultural and religious beliefs pertaining, may take possession of an individual. Possession has been recognised as a marked change in behaviour of the possessed person and exorcism has been regarded as the appropriate procedure to remedy the condition. Such belief was clearly prevalent during Jesus' time; in St Mark's gospel we read how Jesus cast out such an 'unclean' spirit and restored a demoniac to normal health. He also encouraged his disciples to do likewise.

By the twentieth century at least some denominations of the Christian Church were clearly uncomfortable with the idea of exorcism. In 1976 a working party of the Church of Scotland recommended that the Church should have nothing to do with exorcism, which could do more harm than good. This attitude seems a little inconsistent with what one reads in St Mark's gospel, but I am unqualified to comment further. As I understand it, the current situation with regard to the Anglican Church is that every Diocese has a priest who is designated to serve as an exorcist should the need arise. However, I am ignorant as to how often the powers of the exorcist are called upon or how frequently they are effective.

I shall now give an account of an event in which my father played a prominent, not to say vital, role in the restoration of the mental health of one of my maternal aunts. The malady had some of the characteristics of 'Multiple Personality Disorder'. My mother's sister F was unhappily married to someone who drank too much and who treated her badly. My mother came to hear that F was now very ill. In fact she had suddenly turned from a mild and rather timid woman into someone who now terrified her husband. While this change might have been considered to be for the better it was apparent that she was also hostile to all the members of her family and this change in her personality disturbed all of them. My father and mother decided to visit F and as they drove up in the car my father suddenly said, "I think that I could cure F." He told me years afterwards that he did not know why he said this but events proved him right. When they arrived at F's house she confronted my father. She had an expression of fury and hatred on her face and she said, "I know why you have come and you are not going to do it." My father said that he felt that he had to get hold of F's hands in his own. He seized them both and F struggled briefly. She then turned to my parents as though she were seeing them for the first time and then said, in a tone of voice that they all knew well, "Hello Dolly. Hello Billy." The reversion to her former personality was sudden, complete, and irreversible; much to everyone's relief, especially that of her husband. She told them that the last thing she remembered was standing in the kitchen saying to herself that she was so unhappy that she really did not care what happened to her. My father told F's husband that her illness had been his fault. He agreed and swore that he would not drink again or maltreat his wife. Regrettably he did not keep his promises and he returned to drink. He died of a stroke not long afterwards.

It seems difficult, in the 21st century to take this account of apparent possession seriously and I would forgive the reader for dismissing it out of hand as no more than an uncorroborated fabrication on my part. However, similar cases have been reported (the well-known example that became the subject of a book and then of a film 'The Exorcist' is only one of a number in the literature, including the several examples in the Gospels.) In his book *Human Personality and its Survival of Bodily Death,* Fredric Myers discusses whether such cases of possession, or secondary personality, are truly explicable in terms of a foreign entity taking over the body of the possessed or whether the secondary personality is no more than another fragment-or another synthesis of the afflicted individual.

It is evident that a case for 'possession' actually being the taking over of the body of one individual by the personality of another is greatly strengthened if the new personality shows knowledge of verifiable facts, not known previously to the person possessed but known to the possessing entity. The essential features of such a case, first published in the Religio-Philosophical Journal, Chicago in 1879, are described in a book by Professor Ducasse *A Critical Examination of The Belief in Life after Death.* (27). The original report was made by Dr E. Winchester Stevens who was closely involved with the families affected. It concerns the apparent possession of a 13 year old girl, Lurancy Vennum, by another girl, Mary Roff who had died, aged 18, just 14 months after Lurancy was born. During the phase of possession, which lasted over three months, Lurancy claimed that she was Mary Roff. She became so home sick that her family agreed to her moving into the Roff home. Here she was able to relate hundreds of details of the life of Mary Roff and recognised and could name those who were friends and neighbours of the Roff family in the years preceding Lurancy's birth. She also recalled details of a journey that Mary and other members of the Roff family had made to Texas 7 years before Lurancy's birth. In contrast, she did not recognise any of the Vennum family. In this regard it may be noted that contact between the Roff and Vennum families prior to Lurancy's possession was very slight.

Taken at face value this case provides evidence not only of possession but also of the survival of the personality of Mary Roff, complete with her childhood and teenage memories and family affections. An alternative explanation, based on the view that Lurancy simply acted the role of Mary (whom she could not have met in the flesh after Lurancy herself was more than 14 months old) and that she acquired all her detailed knowledge of Mary's life telepathically from her living relatives, while not strictly inadmissible, does demand much of Lurancy's ability to maintain the same role without error for 3 months and to have an altogether remarkable telepathic gift.

More recent evidence from cases of multiple personality has supported the suggestion of Fredric Myers, already alluded to, that these arise from the subconscious mind of the sufferers. For a review see Ian Wilson *Mind out of Time?* (28). One characteristic of these cases is that, as with my aunt, on its reappearance the original personality has no recollection of what transpires during the time that another personality is in control. In my aunt's case there was a clear advantage in her becoming, by whatever means, transformed from a meek and bullied woman into an aggressive one who dominated her husband. Given the capacity of human imagination to create entirely credible fictitious characters it would be unwise to ascribe my aunt's possession to anything more than an unconscious synthesis of the personality that, in part at least, she wished to become. As with my aunt F, a trigger for the development of the multiple personalities that Wilson described is a stressful situation from which the sufferer can find no normal means of escape. However, whether all multiple personalities fall into this category I do not regard as incontrovertible. The Vennum/Roff case already outlined argues against the idea. Further, I have already described how my brother Jack, shot down after a raid on Germany, apparently took over my mother's physical body in order to convince my father that he was still alive. The reader will recall that the authenticity of the communication was established beyond any reasonable doubt by the fact that my brother was able to give a piece of information, subsequently verified, that was totally unknown to either of my parents. Pertinent to the current discussion, among the last words spoken by 'Jack' to my father was "I've got to go now." This may be taken to indicate that the take over, or possession, was only permitted for a brief interval of time. Whether it was my mother's psyche, wishing to take over once again the body it normally possessed, that drew the interaction to an end I cannot say. Neither do I know the factors that brought about the end of the possession of Lurancy Vennum by Mary Roff. However, if it is valid to suppose that in my aunt's case she was possessed by a malevolent entity that was not of her making, then it would seem that she did not have the strength to expel it herself, but that my father did.

It is evident that in a subject like multiple personality, in which we have no scientifically established 'laws of nature' and where consequently, it is difficult to formulate agreed working definitions, there is ample scope for confusion. In a recent television programme, where a priest was ostensibly demonstrating exorcism it was difficult to avoid the impression that the so-called possession was in reality a hypnotic suggestion unintentionally given to the subject by the exorcist himself. However, the account that I have given of the essentially instantaneous cure of the very real malady of my aunt by my father has an even more remarkable precedent in the literature. In their book *Phantasms of the Living* (21), the authors report on a very well documented case (#285) in which the then Officer of Health in the Hellenic army cured a violent and severely deranged young man simple by seizing him by the arm. The man had been ill for five years and no doctor had been successful in treating him hitherto. This case was made even more remarkable by the fact that the Office of Health who affected the cure had a prior auditory hallucination calling on him to 'Go to Volterra'. At this time M. Volterra was completely unknown to the Officer of Health, but it transpired that Volterra was the name of the deranged young man. There are clear similarities between this case and the one that I have just described concerning my aunt. In both cases the affected person tried initially to attack the 'exorcist' only to revert to normal a short time later when the would-be attacker was physically overwhelmed. One could well believe that in earlier times these events would have been regarded as the casting out of 'unclean spirits'.

I can only end this section by concluding that, whereas many cases of multiple personality are probably no more than manifestations of products of the afflicted individual's own mind, I have reservations about this being always the case. While it may be unattractive to retain this reservation, I believe that the evidence requires it.

A mystical experience

My wife Mahalla and I were married in 1961 and our first son, Donnie, was born in May 1965. The birth was difficult but the outcome was all that his parents could have wished for. Donnie was a delightful child who gave much joy to his grandparents as well as to his mother and father. For the first year and a half of his life our son grew well and passed all his developmental milestones easily. However, he then became pale and lacking in energy and our doctor diagnosed anaemia for which he prescribed iron tablets. It was soon evident that the treatment was having no effect and Donnie was admitted to the major hospital in the area for further examination. At the end of these investigations Mahalla and I were invited into the office of the paediatric houseman who asked a long series of questions. These questions were disturbing but it was not until the consultant came into the room that we were told that Donnie had leukaemia. I think by that time we had strong suspicions about the nature of Donnie's illness but the confirmation was grim. The consultant offered a small consolation. With appropriate drug treatment a remission would be induced but ultimately the disease would recur and after a second final remission the subsequent relapse would not respond to therapy. The consultant then told us that in the medical literature there were described about 250 cases where a permanent cure had occurred. There was therefore a very slim chance that our son would not relapse after the induction of the remission.

The course of Donnie's illness was very much as the consultant had predicted (cure rates of acute lymphoblastic leukaemia in children are much higher now than they were forty years ago and the great majority survive). Donnie lived for another eighteen months during which time his brother Jack was born. Donnie was clearly delighted with his young brother who was a most undemanding child – a characteristic for which his parents were most grateful. As Donnie's illness entered it terminal phase Mahalla, Jack and I were allowed to sleep in the hospital in a spare room near our sick son. On his last day, as Mahalla and I stood by his bed Mahalla suggested that I should lie down for a while as I looked very tired. As much as anything to please her, I did so. I did not sleep but after half-an-hour got up with the intention of returning to the ward. At that moment, and quite unexpectedly I had an overpowering feeling of being deeply loved. This feeling, which seemed to fill the room, lasted for a short time and then faded quite quickly. I have read similar accounts by others who have also found it impossible to convey in words the nature of their experience. After this brief episode I returned to the ward and Donnie died five minutes later. His last words were "Keep the door open."

Discussion of the Preceding Accounts of the Paranormal

Given the parents that I had, already as a child I was aware that a materialistic interpretation of our existence is totally inadequate to describe what we are. Running through this account are records of events that have convinced me that the physical world is only one aspect of the totality of reality. Of course the accounts that I have given of paranormal phenomena are of no evidential value in support of their validity. Nothing of what I have written is supported by sworn affidavits of independent witnesses and in many cases it would have been virtually impossible to obtain such documentation. However, I am not writing this to convince the sceptic. There is ample evidence for hypnosis, telepathy, seeing-at-a-distance, and, more controversially, communication between the living and the 'dead' already in the literature. Because this last point has such great implications for all of us I shall say a little more. Those who have made a lifelong study of the paranormal emphasise the practical difficulties of establishing the existence of life after death. To illustrate the nature of the difficulty that these investigators encounter we may consider the case of Brenda Nash described above. The most direct interpretation of that paranormal event is that after Brenda's murder her spirit was able to temporarily take over my mother's body and to express her distress. My mother being able to see the site where Brenda's body lay would appear to be an example of seeing-at-a-distance in the same way that my mother had 'seen' the warning wire in Jack's POW camp. While I believe this interpretation to be the correct one it is not possible to totally exclude that my mother telepathically picked up the distress of Brenda's relatives and her unconscious mind attributed this input to a communication with Brenda herself. I do not find this suggestion attractive because at the séance in which Brenda spoke my mother manifested Brenda's distress as though it were a first-person experience. Similarly, when my brother Jack communicated, via my mother, to my father after being shot down returning from a raid on Germany the way my mother acted and spoke was much more characteristic of Jack himself than it was of my mother. Now, whereas Brenda Nash was dead at the time of her control of my mother, Jack was alive. The most economical conclusion that one can draw from this similarity is that, as far as the control of a sensitive is concerned it is of no consequence whether the controlling entity is living or dead. If this is so, then the relative rarity of instances

67

where the control is a living person (I do not know of another example, but I have been told that they do exist) may simply be a consequence of the fact that there are usually alternative, and less difficult ways for living people to communicate with one another.

Frederic Myers, in his book Human Personality and its Survival of Bodily Death, states:

> *...that in Possession* (now commonly called 'Control') *the automatist's own personality does for a time altogether disappear, while there is a more or less complete substitution of personality; writing or speech being given by a spirit through the entranced organism. There has recently been a great accretion of evidence in this direction. The result broadly is that the phenomena of possession* (note that Myers uses the word 'possession' without any implication that the entity involved is in any way malignant) *are now the most amply attested, as well as intrinsically advanced in our whole repertoire. ..... The controlling spirit proves his identity mainly by reproducing, in speech or writing, facts which belong to his memory and not to the automatist's memory. He may also give evidence of supernormal perceptions of other kinds.* (3c)

It will be seen that Jack's control of my mother is compatible with this assertion and alternative explanations seem rather more unlikely than the one Myers proposes. Similarly, the mode of communication between my father and Brenda Nash certainly had all the appearance of a temporary control of my mother's physical self with the spirit of the victim. In his exemplary critical book 'Psychical Research, the science of the super-normal' Hans Driesch, onetime Professor of Philosophy at the University of Leipzig, says, of paranormal communications:

> *When the content of these communications is alleged to come from a deceased person .. (and when thought – reading from a person present is excluded),...this content is almost always confined to the actual and latent knowledge possessed by this particular deceased person during his lifetime; and in many well-established cases the medium did not know the deceased. Further, it often happens that the communications far transgress the degree of culture of the medium, while they conform to that of the alleged*

spirit. Moreover they often contain examples of the deceased person's form of expressing himself, special ways of talking, nicknames, and other mannerisms of his unknown to the medium. Driesch, ever cautious, says that these observations ...... *can be thrown into the balance in favour of a monadic (survival) theory, even if they do not definitely affirm it. These things are often observed and thus are not so extraordinary and unusual.* (29a).

With regard to 'Ruth' several questions might be raised. Was Ruth really a young girl who died in the reign of Elizabeth I ? Might she not instead have been generated within my mother's unconscious mind? Could my mother have learned telepathically about the existence of Fulford from someone who was alive in my parents' time? It is the nature of much of paranormal evidence for survival that questions of this sort can be raised? These possible alternative explanations cannot formally be dismissed when one recognises that telepathy and seeing-at-a-distance can, and do, occur. I doubt whether Ruth would have gone far in convincing Hans Driesch of her existence and, where other cases for survival are much stronger, nothing is lost, except possibly Ruth's composure, by recognising this fact.

In my own view the control of my mother by my brother Jack and by Brenda Nash are most compatible with Myer's assertion that certain individuals have the capacity to temporarily allow other persons to take over their physical body and I find it difficult to dismiss the idea that such temporary control can be exercised by someone who has passed over. As the archives of the Society for Psychical Research will witness, there are ample well-testified examples that support this belief. However, it is evident that given the existence of telepathy and of the capacity of 'sensitives' to see-at-a distance there are only rare circumstances where these phenomena cannot be evoked to explain apparent communications between the living and the 'dead'. For example, the description of my father's uncle Theophilus and the discovery of his name by my mother could be explained in terms of an unconscious telepathic communication between my parents.

Similar difficulties may be encountered in the literature. In one case, recounted in the classic book by Frederic W. H. Myers (3d) a brother and sister devised a test of survival. In a location that was not told to the sister the brother concealed a small item some time before his death and he gave her a sealed envelope containing a message. The aim was to determine whether the whereabouts of the hidden item and the nature of the message in the envelope could be conveyed paranormally by the brother to his sister after his death. The test was completely successful. The difficulty in interpretation is of course, that in principle at least the brother could have conveyed the vital information telepathically to his sister while he was still alive.

However, there is at least one famous instance where it would be very difficult to evoke telepathy between living individuals to explain what appears to be communication between the living and those who have died. For an account of the 'Cross-correspondences' see for example the book already mentioned, by A. Ellison (2d). Note that Driesch, in his appraisal of this case in his own book (29b) points out that the evidence for survival, even in this case, could in principle be explained by telepathy between the sensitives involved. While this is true, such an explanation has to assume that the sensitives subconsciously devised a scheme that called upon them to paranormally acquire the ability to formulate intricate puzzles whose solutions required a knowledge of classical Greek literature. The Cross-correspondence experiments went on some 30 years and were successful even when none of the sensitives involved had any knowledge of classical Greek. If we reject the telepathy hypothesis on the grounds of its extreme intrinsic improbability, then we seem forced to conclude that Myers, Gurney and Sigwick, the deceased communicators of the puzzles, devised them posthumously and conveyed them to the sensitive recipients.

Scepticism and Fraud

In his book 'The Conscious Universe' Dean Radin devotes a whole chapter to Scepticism (20). For anyone wishing to discover why the paranormal is not more widely recognised, this chapter is a good place to begin. The chapter demonstrates the complete failure of those who steadfastly deny the existence of the paranormal to find fault with the very extensive series of well-controlled experiments that have been carried out over the last few decades. One quotation from Radin's book will illustrate the nature of the problem.

70

Parascience has all the qualities of a magical system while wearing the mantle of science. Until significant discoveries are made, science can justifiably ignore it, but it is important to say why: parascience is a pseudo-scientific system of untested beliefs steeped in illusion, error and fraud.

It seems that the author of this statement is demanding scientific proof of the paranormal while saying that *until this is forthcoming* (my italics) science can ignore it. The logical inconsistency is apparent, as is the lack of any evidence to support the claims that all the results of paranormal research can be dismissed as "illusion, error and fraud."

Despite the vast amount of scientific evidence for the paranormal, particularly with regard to the existence of telepathy and 'seeing-at-a-distance' where the nature of the phenomena lend themselves to laboratory investigation and statistical analysis, such phenomena are largely ignored by many (but not all) scientists. The reason is that they challenge the view that the world and our own existence in it can be described entirely in mechanistic terms, essentially in the same way that the tides on earth can be accounted for by the gravitational attraction of the sun and moon. Lack of objectivity can be so deeply ingrained that a sceptic may be quite unaware of it. The acronym ESP (extra-sensory perception) has been regarded as standing for 'error some place' by a scientist who could find no materialistic explanation for this phenomenon. Such prejudice among scientists goes back for at least 100 years.

It is not difficult to find examples of the way that the materialistic paradigm has been protected by the selective reporting of the achievements of those who have been open-minded enough to explore the paranormal. As mentioned above, in 1930 the Pulitzer prizewinner Upton Sinclair published a book 'Mental Radio' on his experiments on telepathy with his wife. In my copy of The Cambridge Encyclopedia published in 1990 the titles of three of Sinclair's novels are printed. However, 'Mental Radio' is not mentioned despite the fact that Albert Einstein was very impressed by it and that it generated great interest at the time.

As noted above, in their book 'Poltergeists' A Gauld and AD Cornell survey some 500 cases of so-called poltergeist phenomena, including some cases that they have investigated themselves (16).

71

They also devote a whole chapter to a discussion of possible explanations for the data based on natural causes, erroneous observation or recall, deliberate fraud or lying and conspiracy by witnesses. They conclude that in principle all of the phenomena *may* be so explained provided two or more of these factors were operative. As they remark,

> *...such a position is, in a sense quite impregnable. But to assume without supporting evidence, and despite numerous considerations (such as we have advanced above) to the contrary, that they do lie behind them, is to insulate one's beliefs in this sphere from all possibility of modification from cold contact of chastening facts.*

William James makes a similar point with regard to the trance mediumship of Mrs Leonore Piper. He says:

> *The scientist who is confident of 'fraud' here, must remember that in science as much as in common life a hypothesis must receive some positive specification and determination before it can be profitably discussed, and fraud which is no assigned kind of fraud, but simply 'fraud' at large, fraud in abstracto can hardly be regarded as a specially scientific explanation of concrete facts.* (30).

One further remark is warranted; where sceptics try to disprove the evidence for the paranormal they persistently (I almost wrote 'religiously') ignore the great mass of well-authenticated data and refer only to the few cases where fraud has been demonstrated. Their argument would seem to rest on the assumption that the detected cases of fraud were only the tip of the iceberg that actually represented fraud in *all* the cases where evidence for the paranormal has been published. On this issue, and with regard to the existence of extrasensory perception, Professor H J Eysenck, the then chairman of the psychology department at University College, London, wrote in 1957:

> *Unless there is a gigantic conspiracy involving some thirty University departments all over the world, and several hundred highly respected scientists in various fields, many of them hostile*

to the claims of the psychical researchers, the only conclusion the unbiased observer can come to must be that there does exist a small number of people who obtain knowledge existing in other people's minds, or in the outer world, by means as yet unknown to science. (20f).

In his support of extrasensory perception Eysenck has joined the group of serious enquirers who, having studied the evidence with an open mind have concluded that the phenomena are real. Professor H H Price formerly Wykeham Professor of Logic at Oxford has written:

Telepathy is something which ought not to happen at all if the Materialistic theory were true. But it does happen. So there must be something seriously wrong with the Materialistic theory how-ever numerous and imposing the normal *facts which support it may be. (31)*

Similarly Professor C D Broad, onetime Knightsbridge Professor of Moral Philosophy at Cambridge says:

There can be no doubt that the events described happened and were correctly reported; that the odds against chance-coincidence piled up to billions to one; and that the nature of the events, which involved both telepathy and precognition, conflicts with one or more basic limiting principles....

It seems to me fairly plain that the establishment of paranormal precognition requires a radical change in our conception of time, and probably a correlated change in our concept of causation. (31)

The two above quotations were originally from articles written in 1949 but scientists in general remain today as hostile to the idea of extrasensory perception as they were 75 years ago when Upton Sinclair published his book – Mental Radio. In his Introduction he wrote:

It should be obvious that I stand to lose much more than I gain by publishing a book of this sort. Many have urged me not to take the risk. It is the part of prudence not to believe too many

73

new and strange ideas. Some of my Socialist and materialistic friends are going to say- without troubling to read what I have written; "Sinclair has gone in for occultism; he is turning into a mystic in his old age." It is true that I am fifty-one, but I think my mind is not entirely gone; and if what I publish is mysticism, then I do not know how there can be such a thing as science about the human mind.

In some ways the title of Sinclair's book is unfortunate. Whatever he had in mind about the mechanism underlying telepathy we can confidently say that, unlike radio, it does not depend on the transmission of electromagnetic waves. Sinclair himself showed that the success rate of tests of telepathy was not diminished when the distance between 'sender' and receiver' was increased from thirty feet to thirty miles and it is equally unimpeded when an electromagnetic screen is imposed between the sender and the recipient. More recent work, in the Soviet Union has extended the range over which telepathy functions to several thousand miles.

The continued prejudice of the scientific establishment has provoked Brian Josephson, Nobel laureate and the present professor of condensed matter physics at Trinity College Cambridge to react against the editorial bias relating to paranormal research shown by the influential science journal 'Nature'. The history of science illustrates just how durable is an established paradigm but ultimately ideas that are wrong are forced to give way. How long it will be before the existence of the paranormal becomes universally accepted I do not know but I think it is still some way off. Of course, as individuals we have to wait no longer than a lifetime to discover that we survive death.

While modern scientific methodology has excluded fraud and unconscious self-deception as explanations for the paranormal phenomena observed, the lay public do not have the advantages open to the research scientist. In such circumstances cases of fraud are to be anticipated and do occur. Nevertheless, deception can be avoided provided one maintains a healthy degree of scepticism at the outset. I can illustrate this point by an experience of my own.

Some spiritualist acquaintances of mine had heard of a man, I shall call him 'X', who, with an associate 'Y', claimed to materialise flowers out of thin air (apports). Some of my friends attended a demonstration given by 'X' in Manchester and on their return

74

one of them declared confidently that 'X' was "clearly genuine." I did not doubt my friends' honesty but I remained unconvinced about 'X', not least because he demanded that the rooms in which he gave his performances be completely blacked out. With my friends' agreement I invited 'X' to meet us and give a second demonstration. In my invitation I asked 'X' to agree that we should search both him and his associate 'Y' before the demonstration took place. He accepted the invitation, but only on the condition that he should also search us. We agreed to this strange request but he then refused to give us a definite date for his demonstration. On writing to the Society for Psychical Research in London I learned that they too had their doubts about 'X', partly because of what they had discovered regarding the visit of 'X' and 'Y' to Australia where the two mediums had difficulty in giving an unscheduled, and therefore unprepared, demonstration of the materialisation of flowers. We made no further attempt to persuade 'X' to visit us but shortly afterwards his deception was exposed when it was found (by someone switching on the light during a performance) that 'X' concealed the 'materialised' flowers in the battery compartment of the tape recorder that he took with him when giving a demonstration. For myself, I would not attend any demonstration of the paranormal where the phenomenon purported to occur was so photophobic as to require complete darkness for its manifestation.

While deliberate deceptions of this sort are not common they do result in gullible people paying money to those who set out to deceive them. Unfortunately, their fraudulent behaviour serves to undermine the credibility of the great majority of mediums who do not consciously deceive the public. I have to introduce the word 'consciously' here because I feel that there are a very significant number of 'mediums' whose psychical gifts are more limited than they themselves believe them to be. If these 'mediums' give public demonstrations of the paranormal, as many of them do in Spiritualist Churches, then they too might deter anyone seeking evidence for the paranormal.

Despite these caveats some genuine and highly gifted mediums are to be found going the rounds of spiritualist churches. William James made the point that to prove white crows exist it is not necessary to prove all crows are white but only to find one white crow.

Psychic Research and the Christian Religion

Both Old and New Testaments of the Bible contain many accounts of what today we would call paranormal phenomena. Michael Perry, one time Archdeacon of Durham, quoting from the book, *Vision and audition in biblical prophecy as illuminated by recent research in human consciousness*, by B.M. Bennett writes:

> *... when we begin to examine the Bible in terms of the categories of the paranormal, we are confronted with an almost embarrassing abundance of parapsychological riches. For example, telepathy, clairvoyance, precognition, mediumship, psychokinesis and out of body experiences.* Perry goes on to say that *The paranormal and the miraculous are not identical phenomena, though they overlap; to remove either from the pages of the Bible would be to emasculate it intolerably.* (32a).

This being so I find it difficult to understand why orthodox Christianity seems generally to have ignored the scientific study of the paranormal. As Perry writes:

> *Interest in the paranormal as a scientific pursuit has, however, always been a minor concern amongst Christians. The suspicion has been that those who 'dabbled' in such matters were well on the way to slipping down the primrose path to perdition to join the heretics and schismatics for whom no fate was bad enough.* (32b).

To accept this view would seem to suggest that those in Biblical times who 'dabbled' in , *telepathy, clairvoyance, precognition, mediumship, psychokinesis and out of body experiences'* were involved in activities best left alone. Alternatively, one would have to suppose that what was acceptable 2000 years ago is now, for some inexplicable reason, no longer so.

To the scientist this is a disappointing response to the study of those phenomena, among others, that serve to demonstrate that a materialistic view of the world is inadequate to account for all human experience. True religion, like true science, can have nothing to fear from knowledge gained by the sincere pursuit of truth.

Despite my own acceptance of the value of psychical research in expanding my awareness of the spiritual my own religious beliefs do not rest totally on my experience and further knowledge of the paranormal. I shall return to this subject later when I attempt a synthesis of my views.

Reincarnation

It is natural to ask ourselves the questions that children ask. 'Where do we come from and where do we go when we die? If life starts when we are conceived or have reached a state of foetal maturity at which life outside the womb is possible, and finishes when we die, then our existence is merely a very brief transient in cosmological time; one life time is less than ten billionths that of the estimated age of the Universe. Further, as the sun ages it will increase in temperature and expand until its outer atmosphere extends to the orbit of the earth. Long before this all life on earth will perish and all material signs of its human occupancy will disappear. If one accepts such a belief in the brevity of our existence then all human suffering, striving, scientific exploration and artistic creations are no more than a colossal exercise in futility. On the other hand, if there is an essential part of us that survives death then we possess a necessary element in our renunciation of the futility just alluded to. All the major religions propose some final destiny for man in which he reaches some state of ultimate perfection. Recognising that mankind is presently and to varying degrees less than perfect these religions all propose ways whereby man achieves his final state. As I am not a theologian my own understanding of what the various faiths maintain is inevitably less than it would otherwise be. However, as this book is an outline of my own belief I must state such understanding as I have.

Several of the world's major religions, Hinduism, Jainism and Sikhism maintain that in order to attain perfection the soul (the *atman* of the Hindu) is reincarnated on earth an untold number of times until perfection has been achieved. Buddhism also speaks of rebirth but in its doctrine of *anatta* (no soul) it denies the existence of a permanent soul. It is notable, but not surprising that no religion gives a comprehensive description of the final state that follows this attainment.

In contrast to the Eastern religions just referred to Christianity does not accept that the soul exists before conception and maintains that this incarnate life is the only one we have, at least until

77

our resurrection. Depending on how we live our life and on our faith in the redeeming power of the love of Christ, we are either saved or not. Traditionally the unsaved were consigned to everlasting hell and some fundamentalist Christians still hold to this belief. However, modern Christianity as a whole, realising that eternal damnation is not compatible with the belief in a God who loves mankind has moderated its views on the state of unrepentant sinners, but I am unclear what alternative has been put forward.

To quote from a modern philosopher whose roots are in Christianity.

Within Judaism, Christianity and Islam there is the belief that the soul, as the present conscious self, continues to exist after the death of the body, either living forever as a spirit, or being at some stage reunited with its physical body, or acquiring a new 'spiritual' body. The conclusion of the human story, according to these traditions, is eternal life in heaven, or in heaven via an intermediate state, or in hell.

This concept involves immense difficulties, which no doubt accounts for the fact that so many people within the three monotheistic traditions no longer seriously believe it. The faithful echo it in liturgies, hymns and ecclesiastical rhetoric, particularly within funeral services, but it does not, for most, form part of the operative set of convictions by which they live. (33)

If this assertion is correct it is perhaps not surprising that in the West there is now much interest in Hinduism and Buddhism.

Although the concept of reincarnation is now regarded as more or less an exclusively Eastern tradition the historic record shows an interest, not to say a belief, in reincarnation in the West that goes back in the pre-Christian era, most clearly to Plato, and forward into the Christian era with such philosophers as Kant and Schopenhauer. A useful review of the history of the belief in reincarnation, both in Eastern and Western thought is to be found in Ducasse, C.J. (27).

Within Christianity up to the third century at least reincarnation certainly had its proponents. Origen, author of *De Principiis*, the first systematic theology of Christianity, and regarded by St Gregory of Nyssa as the 'prince of Christian learning', wrote

Every soul comes into this world strengthened by the victories or
weakened by the defeats of its previous life. Its place in this world
as a vessel appointed to honour or dishonour, is determined by its
previous merits or demerits. Its work in this world determines its
place in the world which follows this. (34a)

This statement makes clear that Origen believed that the soul
could be made incarnate more than once and he further maintained
that this process was repeated until the soul had achieved that state
of perfection that merited its entry into heaven. However, when
Constantine, the first Christian Roman emperor called the council of Nicea in 325 AD to define Christian orthodoxy, it ruled against
reincarnation. Despite this ruling some Christians, particularly in
Palestine continued to adhere to Origen's teaching and were apparently tolerated by the church until the 6th century. However, the
end for a belief in reincarnation within Christianity effectively came
in 553 AD when emperor Justinian pronounced that anyone assert-
ing the pre-existence of souls would suffer excommunication. In
its response to heresy the early church reacted like any other organ-
isation that maintains and depends on a particular system of belief.
Heresy is a challenge to that belief and predictably evokes a hostile response. One sees the same phenomenon today as parapsychology challenges the materialistic view of many scientists.

The intolerance to the idea of reincarnation of the most powerful in the Christian church of the 4th to 6th centuries ensured
that it did not survive as a belief even among a minority group. Had
it been allowed to do so the picture today might have been much
different, with the great interest evoked in the West by reincarnation teachings from the East. As it is, it seems that Perry is justified in saying:

Those who today try to persuade Christians of the truth of rein-
carnation cannot credibly claim that they are restoring an ancient
Christian doctrine to its true place. They are following in the
wake of idiosyncratic thinkers who were never able to persuade
the bulk of Christianity to their way of looking at things. (32c)

The Search for Evidence of Reincarnation

Just as modern parapsychological research has sought evidence for life after death so too has it enquired as to whether the ancient belief in reincarnation can be either substantiated or refuted.

The routes of enquiry have been as follows:

Déjà vu

Many of us have had the experience of seeing a place or observing an event for the first time but have had at the same time the feeling that the experience has happened before. While such déjà vu might be an indication that the present event is triggering the recollection of a similar one that happened in a previous incarnation the argument can hardly be a compelling one. The neurosurgeon Wilder Pinfield found that some patients, being operated on for epilepsy, reported that they experienced déjà vu when a certain region of the right temporal lobe was electrically stimulated. While it may be argued that this region of the brain is actually activated by the recall of an experience in a previous incarnation and that it is this activation that brings the recall into consciousness, one could not exclude the possibility that this same region is on rare occasions spontaneously activated by some transient neural instability and that this triggers the déjà vu experience. This hypothesis does not exhaust the list of trivial explanations for déjà vu and one must conclude that, given the attendant uncertainties as to the origin of the phenomenon, it contributes little to the discussion of the existence of reincarnation.

Child prodigies

A very small number of children show aptitudes and skills that far exceed those of their peers. Examples can be found in the realms of music, mathematics, the command of languages, and international chess. Children of several nationalities have been so gifted and for some reason the majority, at least of those reported, have been boys. Two well known examples are given below.

Wolfgang Amadeus Mozart the Austrian child musical prodigy, made his first professional tour as a pianist at the age of six years and wrote his first opera at the age of seven.

Several accounts of the early life of Carl Friedrich Gauss, the famous German mathematician establish him as a prodigy. For example, on one occasion, as he walked through a forest with his uncle, he asked whether any trees in the forest had the same number of leaves. His uncle said that he did not know and it would be an impractical task to find out. To which the young Gauss replied "If there are more trees in the forest than there are leaves on a tree, then there must be some trees with the same number of leaves."

Such savants, though rare do continue to be found. One of the most recent, Daniel Tammet, is a UK citizen. It has been shown that he is able to give the value of π to over 20,000 significant figures with no error whatever and can learn enough of the Icelandic language in seven days to be able to converse with two Icelanders on television.

The age at which these unusual gifts appear has on occasion been very early, within the first few years of life. As one would anticipate from the fact that consciousness is not understood there is no scientific explanation for the phenomenon of child prodigies. However, the fact of their existence has been considered by some to be evidence of reincarnation, prodigies being those who have learned a particular skill in a previous incarnation and who recall their knowledge in this life. If this is so, then the recollection seems highly specific as it does not extend to a recall of the past life itself when the enabling knowledge was putatively acquired. This absence of a general recall cannot, of course, be used as an argument to refute the idea of reincarnation and nor can the observation that prodigies are so few. The idea is not new that at birth we bring with us knowledge from a previous existence. Plato (c.427-347 BC) claimed that all knowledge, at least of abstract ideas such as beauty, good, justice, holiness and of mathematics was in fact recollection from a previous life. On this view we all bear witness to a life before birth. Plato further argues his case for reincarnation by saying:

For if the living spring from any others who are not the dead, and they die, must not all things at last be swallowed up in death? (35)

My own view is that we cannot argue for reincarnation simply by our failure to find an alternative explanation for savants. That the existence of prodigies defies our current understanding is without question, but this is true of mental ability in general. There is one man who entertains himself by learning pages of the telephone directory. Certainly the numbers that he learns he is not really recalling from a previous incarnation (unless one wishes to argue, what is certainly true, that our ideas of time are too simplistic). This ability by savants to recall vast numbers of unrelated facts suggests that most of us do not use all of the memory resource available to us. The demonstration that under hypnosis an individual may recall facts that are quite unknown in the normal waking state, (cryptomnesia) suggests that normal consciousness protects us from being aware of memories that are of no use to us, rather than that those memories do not exist.

Age regression under hypnosis

Attempts have been made to establish evidence for reincarnation by the most direct approach – to find individuals who have memories of a past life and can, from those memories furnish verifiable information that is virtually inaccessible to them in their current state. In some studies hypnosis has been used as a way of facilitating such recall. The method seems deceptively simple but is fraught with difficulties. A hypnotised subject, invited to recall a past life is very likely to oblige. Given the ability of fiction writers to invent characters who may strongly engage our interest, the ability of hypnotised subjects to describe past lives, whether real or imaginary, is not surprising. In many cases no verifiable information, that was unknown to the subject before hypnosis, is forthcoming and in some instances the recalled previous life seems only to demonstrate the impressive ability of the subject to create a plausible life from a combination of vivid imagination buttressed by the remembering of apparently forgotten facts acquired during the 'current' incarnation of the subject (cryptomnesia). An example is given below which amply justify this caveat.

In 1969 a Cardiff housewife, Jane Evans (a pseudonym) was treated for rheumatism by a hypnotherapist, Arnall Bloxham. On being asked, under hypnosis to regress back in time she gave details of six previous lives, two of which were rich with verifiable historic detail. In one she recalled being Livonia, the wife of a tutor to a Roman family living in Eboracum, the Roman name for York, in the fourth century AD. She gave a several details which were historically correct and others which, while not verifiable, were at least judged plausible by historians. Further, she mentioned four characters with plausible Roman names but for whom no historic record has come down to us. Livonia spoke just as though she were actually witnessing the events in front of her eyes and conveyed her emotional reaction to them. All these details generated great interest in the idea of reincarnation, and became the subject of a BBC TV programme, 'The Bloxham Tapes' in 1976, and subsequently of a book *More Lives than One*, by the programme producer Jeffrey Iverson. However, while this case initially seemed to present support for reincarnation, evidence was forthcoming that cryptomnesia was the source of the apparent recall of a previous existence (24b). A historic novel by Louis de Wohl, published in 1947 was discovered that described in detail the fictional event that 'Livonia' had recounted to Arnall Bloxham. Significantly, the names of four of the fictional characters in this book were the same as the four recalled by 'Livonia' who were not known from historical records. Finally, in de Wohl's book the Roman town of Verulamium was shortened to Verulam and 'Livonia' had used precisely the same abbreviation.

As Ian Wilson describes in his book, investigation of the other recollections of previous lives by Jane Evans revealed historic inaccuracies and one has to conclude that the hypnotically induced 'age regressions' that she underwent really demonstrated how remarkably a hypnotised subject is able to trawl through their repository of hidden memories to satisfy the request of the hypnotist. While one would not be justified, a priori, in dismissing all hypnotic regression evidence of reincarnation in this way there is clearly a need for caution.

A second example of a hypnotically induced age regression that resulted in the apparent recall of a previous life is the well known Bridey Murphy case. In 1956 an American businessman, Morey Bernstein published his best selling book 'The Search for Bridey Murphy'. Here he described the results that he had obtained using age regression hypnosis with a 29 year old Colorado housewife, Virginia Tighe. Under hypnosis Virginia described her previous life in nineteenth century Ireland as one Bridey Murphy. She gave detailed information about her home in Cork, her marriage, her subsequent move to Belfast and she showed knowledge of the Irish customs of the day and used words that were current in Ireland in the late 18th century but have become obsolete since. In particular she mentioned making purchases from two grocers in Belfast called Farr and John Carrigan. It was claimed that as Virginia Tighe she had no access to the knowledge that as Bridey Murphy she displayed of Ireland. While, as discussed below, this case could do no more than suggest reincarnation as a possible explanation, the actual facts became controversial. An American newspaper, the Chicago American, managed to discover the true identity of Bernstein's hypnotised subject (in his book Bernstein had used a pseudonym, Ruth Simmons to conceal Virginia Tighe's identity) and revealed that Virginia had spent some of her childhood in Chicago. The newspaper claimed that she had lived there with an Irish aunt who was 'as Irish as the lakes of Killarney' and who, by implication, might well have been the source of much of Virginia's knowledge of Ireland. It turned out that these allegations were untrue. Virginia *had* lived in Chicago in her late teens where she had an aunt of Scots-Irish extraction who had been born in New York. Other claims made by the newspaper were also untrue and revealed the readiness of the paper to use misinformation to devalue the evidence for reincarnation afforded by the case. The allegation that in Chicago Virginia had known a Mrs Bridie Murphy Corkell was not substantiated. Mrs Bridie Corkell, although a real person, proved very elusive and there was no evidence that her name had ever been Murphy. What was established however, was that Mrs Corkell was the mother of the editor of the Chicago American, the newspaper that claimed to have exposed Bridey Murphy as a hoax.

Professor Ducasse, in his very detailed review of the case (36) stripped it of the misinformation that had been used to discredit it, and concluded that it provided fairly strong evidence that under hypnosis Virginia Tighe was able to acquire detailed information paranormally of obscure facts relating to 19th century Ireland. However, as Ducasse stressed, such acquisition could not prove that she was a reincarnation of 'Bridey Murphy'. Such proof would demand that all normal and all other paranormal means of obtaining the information be excluded and that a real Bridey Murphy could be discovered in historic records.

More cases of hypnosis-induced recall of past lives are described in the book The Case for Reincarnation by J Fisher (34b). One concerns a Norfolk teacher, Margaret Baker, who under hypnosis recalled a previous life as a gypsy horse dealer Tyzo Boswell. As Boswell she spoke in a coarse, guttural language and was suspicious of her *gorgio* (non-gypsy) interviewer who was a hypnotherapist called Maurice Blake. She described 'her' life as Tyzo from 1775 until his untimely death by being struck by lightning at Horncastle fair, in Lincolnshire, in 1831. After the regression Margaret, who had no recollection of what she had said under hypnosis, was astonished to learn that she had been a man in her previous incarnation and was no doubt surprised to hear how 'she' had died.

Subsequent to this regression Margaret Baker visited the graveyard of St Mary's Church, Tetford, in Lincolnshire where the grave of Tyzo Boswell is situated. The tombstone records that Boswell died by being struck by lightening on August 5, 1831 and the parish register shows that he was buried two days later. Margaret said that although she had never been to the area before she felt great familiarity with it and knew exactly where the tombstone was. Neither she nor Maurice Blake had any contact with gypsies but in her regression she used several Romany words, such as 'motto'- drunk, 'mello'- dead and 'chopping greis' meaning selling horses, all of which were subsequently found to be authentic.

While the details revealed by the regression are impressive, like all regression cases it can do no more than suggest reincarnation. It is simply not possible to exclude that Margaret Baker actually acquired her information by other means, either by cryptomnesia or even paranormally by telepathy or seeing-at-a-distance. From Fisher's book one cannot discover whether there is evidence that the Tyzo Boswell buried at Tetford was actually a gypsy. Unless this is forthcoming one might suggest that part of Margaret Baker's regression was based on a real, but 'forgotten' knowledge that a man buried at Tetford died by being struck by lightening while the rest was an invention of Margaret's unconscious mind. Such inventiveness is not unknown as the case of Jane Evans, described above illustrates. While these alternative explanations may not be very likely it may be difficult to rule them out. We cannot demand more from the evidence than it is capable of giving us.

Evidence of reincarnation from children

The best evidence for reincarnation is to be found in children who spontaneously claim that they recall previous lives. The earliest recorded case, from Japan, is nearly 200 years old (20) but a systematic search by Ian Stephenson has brought to light many more of 20th century origin of which no less than one third were from the USA or UK (37a). Here I record a small sample from the available literature as an illustration of the phenomenon.

Alexandrina Samona (27)

This well documented case occurred in 1910 and concerned a doctor and his family who lived in Parlermo, Sicily. Dr Carmelo Samona and his wife Adela had a daughter Alexandrina who died at the age of five in the March of that year. Three days after her death her mother dreamed that her daughter came to her and told her that she was not far away and would be reborn to her. The same dream recurred three days later. Mme Samona told a friend of her dreams and the latter suggested that they meant that Alexandrina would be reincarnated and born again to her mother.

The mother rejected the dreams, not least because she had had an operation that she believed would prevent her having any more children. Some days later, when Mme. Samona was expressing to her husband her heartfelt grief over the loss of their daughter three sharp knocks were heard (parenthetically, it is notable that just such a series of raps were heard by my father when he was seeking evidence for the survival of his grandfather (see page 59)). Following this experience the parents decided to hold séances to see whether they could obtain further information. The very first séance was successful in that two spirits, one claiming to be Alexandrina herself and the other an aunt who had died many years before communicated with the parents. 'Alexandrina' told her parents that it was she who had appeared in her mother's dreams and she was responsible for the three loud knocks. She further said that she would be reborn before Christmas and that she would come with a twin sister. In subsequent séances 'Alexandrina' repeatedly insisted that this communication be passed on to relations and friends of the family.

In November 1910 Mme. Samona gave birth to twin daughters, one of whom resembled Alexandrina in several distinctive ways: with regard to physical appearance, temperament, behaviour and interests and even her marked aversion to cheese (see Table below). She was given the same name as her sister who had died.

When the twins were ten years old they were told that the family were to make a trip to Montreale, a place that they had not visited before. Alexandrina II claimed that she had been there before in the company of a lady "who had horns". She recalled seeing priests there in red robes and described the large statue on top of the church. Mme Samona remembered that some months before Alexandrina I had died she had taken her to Montreale where they had seen a number of young Greek priests who were wearing blue cloaks trimmed with red. Accompanying the child and her mother on their visit was a lady with benign outgrowths (sebaceous cysts) on her head.

The value of the case is much enhanced by the fact that the parents had followed the wishes of Alexandrina I, expressed during the séances, that they should tell others of her forthcoming rebirth. These individuals, who included an Evangelical pastor, attested to the facts. Further, Mme Samona's friend confirmed that she had been told, in March 1910, of the dreams in which Alexandrina had informed her mother of her return.

The case is atypical in as much as the apparent rebirth of Alexandrina was announced paranormally in advance of the event. However, it is not unique in the fact that the rebirth occurred to the same family as the one previously bereaved (38).

Assessment of the case of Samona

To what extent the Samona case supports the concept of reincarnation depends on how convincingly one can dismiss alternative explanations for the events purported to have occurred. Given the number of individuals who attested to the fact that 'Alexandrina' foretold her rebirth I believe that fraud can be reasonably excluded. Of course it is possible that for some reason all the witnesses colluded to concoct the whole story. In any one instance of the occurrence of an unusual event one must entertain the idea that fraud is involved, and as we have seen, claims of fraud have commonly been used to discount phenomena that run counter to established belief. However, in the Samona case a claim of fraud does not sit well with the fact that the attesters were not solely the parents of Alexandrina, or even close relatives.

The exclusion of fraud does not exhaust possible explanations that do not require reincarnation. In principle the dreams of

Alexandrina's mother might have been an unconscious expression of her undoubted desire to have her daughter restored to her. To propose such an explanation would require that the dreams were precognitive as far as the birth was concerned and that the mother's unconscious mind presented the precognition in terms of the rebirth of her dead daughter. There is too much special pleading to make this explanation attractive but that does not permit its exclusion.

The results of the séances are also not readily explained. If one grant that the dead daughter could communicate with the mother paranormally one would have to suppose that she deliberately deceived her parents as to the identity of the child that the mother was yet to have born to her by claiming the child would actually be herself. Alternatively one may suggest that the mother conveyed to the members of the séance information about the birth that she had acquired by precognition and that she unconsciously distorted this information in such a way as to make it appear that the dead child was communicating details of her own forthcoming birth.

The similarities between Alexandrina I and II are set out in the following table:

Feature or characteristic	Alexandrina I	Alexandrina II	Other twin
Active, restless and gregarious	No	No	Yes
Content to play alone	Yes	Yes	No
Enjoyed folding cloths or linen and tidying them	Yes	Yes	No
Insisted on having clean hands	Yes	Yes	No
Strong dislike of cheese	Yes	Yes	No
Left-handed	Yes	Yes	Not reported
Noticeable facial asymmetry	Yes	Yes	No
Hyperaemia of left eye	Yes	Yes	No

No single one of these similarities is particularly striking but taken together they carry some weight. The facial asymmetry is reminiscent of other childhood cases of purported reincarnation where a birthmark similar to that possessed by the dead child is found on the 'reincarnated' one (38). All that one can say about the behavioural similarities between the two Alexandrinas is that they are compatible with reincarnation but by no means require it.

As an alternative to postulating reincarnation one may attempt to explain the knowledge that Alexandrina II had about Montreale either by assuming that she obtained it telepathically from her mother or even simply that she remembered hearing her mother talk about it but that her mother had forgotten that she had done so. Both of these suppositions would require either conscious or unconscious deception by the child of her mother because she claimed that she was recalling a personal experience of her own life as Alexandrina I rather than that she was recounting information that she had received from another person.

Overall one may summarise the case by saying that, at the very least it supports the concept of survival and precognition. To the extent it provides evidence for reincarnation depends largely on the weight one gives to the similarities tabulated above and to the readiness with which one is willing to reject the rather tortuous alternative explanations of the dreams and the séances. What the case lacks is a wealth of veridical information that Alexandrina II could recall from her life as Alexandrina I and that was unknown to her mother or other members of her family. The following cases do not suffer from this deficiency.

Shanti Devi

This is a very well known case that is recounted in several sources. Its original documentation depends on the statements made in a pamphlet published in 1936 by three public figures in India (27).

Kumari Shanti Devi, the daughter of B. Rang Bahadur Mathur, was born in October 1926 in Delhi. From the age of four she began to claim that she remembered a previous life in Muttra, a town about 100 miles from Delhi and she gave several very specific details about it: that she had been married to a cloth merchant, that her house had been painted yellow and that her caste had been Choban. Further, she told her grand-uncle that in Muttra her husband's name was Pt. Kedar Nath Chaubey. The granduncle mentioned this to Mr Lala Kishan Chand, M.A., a retired principal, who then met Shanti Devi. At this meeting she gave him the address of her 'husband' in Muttra and Kishan Chand wrote to that address. No doubt to his surprise he received a reply from one Kedar Nath Chaubey and it confirmed the details that Shanti Devi had told the granduncle. In the letter Kedar Nath suggested that a relative of his, Pt. Kanji Mal, who lived in Delhi, should visit Shanti Devi. When they met she recognised him as a cousin of her 'husband' in Muttra and gave him convincing answers to the very specific questions that he asked.

In 1935, when Shanti Devi was just nine years old Pt. Kedar Nath Chaubey visited Delhi with his present wife and with his ten year old son by his former wife. This was an emotional encounter for Shanti Devi who recognised Kedar Nath as her former husband. She was able to answer correctly various questions about her private life as his wife and she mentioned that she had buried Rs. 150 in a certain room in her home in Muttra.

Shortly after the visit to Delhi of Kedar Nath Chaubey and his wife and in response to repeated pleas by Shanti Devi to be taken to Muttra, her parents and the three attesters mentioned above took her there by train. On the railway platform in Muttra Shanti Devi recognised, among a group of people, the elder brother of her former husband and later on in her visit she picked out her own parents among a crowd of more than fifty people and named them correctly.

On leaving the railway station by carriage Shanti Devi was able to direct the adults who had accompanied her from Delhi to both of her former residences in Muttra and gave very precise information about both of them. In addition, near the first she identified an old Brahmin as the father of her former husband and at the second, which was the one that was currently occupied by Kedar Nath and his family, she recognised her former brother. She mentioned that when she had lived there the courtyard had a well and she pointed out correctly where it had been. Further, when a search was made for the cache in which Shanti Devi had claimed she had deposited the Rs. 150 it was found under the floor of one of the rooms precisely as she had indicated. It was now found to be empty but subsequently Kedar Nath explained that he had removed the money after his first wife Lugdi died 10 years earlier, in October 1925, soon after giving birth to a son.

The three authors of the pamphlet describing the case included in their publication a testimony from Kenji Mal, who had interviewed Shanti Devi in Delhi at the request of his cousin Kedar

Nath. This testimony contained the questions that Shanti Devi had been asked and the answers that she had given.

Assessment of the case of Shanti Devi

We may raise the possibility of fraud only to dismiss it with some confidence. If the facts in the pamphlet had been the invention of its authors there were many individuals mentioned in it who could have refuted it. To suppose, instead, that there was a conspiracy of all the others who were involved would have called for a very elaborate scheme requiring the cooperation of two different families. The conspiracy would have had to be sufficiently convincing to deceive the three authors of the pamphlet who were not members of either family and it would have demanded consummate acting skills by a nine-year-old child who could have rehearsed her role only if it were done so in secret. Consequently, if we are to reject reincarnation as an explanation for the detailed and intimate knowledge that Shanti Devi had of the life of the young woman Lugdi, who had lived in a town some one hundred miles from Delhi and who had died a year before Shanti Devi was born, then we have to find an alternative explanation. It is not credible to believe that Shanti Devi acquired this information herself by any normal means because some of it, like the cache beneath the floor in the home of Kedar Nath, was known to only very few individuals and it would also be difficult to account for the fact that during her visit to Muttra she had spoken with the local dialect.

As with the case of Alexandrina Samona it seems unavoidable to conclude that either the case of Shanti Devi is an example of reincarnation or that some paranormal explanation has to be accepted. All the facts that Shanti Devi expounded were known by at least one other person so that if one supposes that the child could tap into all of it telepathically then one might attempt to refute the explanation based on reincarnation. This so-called super ESP hypothesis would require a greater level of telepathic information-gathering than one can normally demonstrate (37) and the child, when confronted with putatively her former husband and her own ten year old son did not behave as though she was simply the recipient of telepathic information that had no emotional content for her.

In his discussion of the Katsugoro case, which shows many similarities to the Shanti Devi one, Professor Ducasse considers

91

the possibility of paranormal retrocognition as being an alternative explanation to that of reincarnation (27). Neither that case nor the Shanti Devi one are characteristic of retrocognition as commonly experienced since the phenomenon manifests itself as a relatively brief hallucination of some historic episode in which one is a spectator rather than a participant. One may contrast such an experience with those of Shanti Devi who remembered veridical episodes that had happened in the past but who did not report having hallucinations of them.

Eduardo Esplugus-Cabrera (38)

Eduardo lived with his parents in Havana and from the age of four he claimed that he had lived a previous life in that city. He gave his previous address as 69 Rue Campanario, his parents names as Pierro and Amparo Seca and his own name as Pancho. He said that his mother had a very clear complexion and black hair and that she made hats. He recalled that he had two brothers Mercedes and Jean and that he bought drugs at a nearby American chemists. He said at the age of thirteen he had left that house for the last time. The date was Sunday, 28th February 1903 and he said that his mother had cried a great deal on that day.

The parents of Eduardo were sure that their four year old son had never been to the house that he had described as it was quite unfamiliar to them. However, to examine his claim they took him there by a very circuitous route. On arrival at Rue Campanario Eduardo picked out the house at once but he failed to recognise its occupants. Inquires locally by the parents elicited the following facts: until some short time after February 1903, 69 Rue Campanario had been occupied by Antonio Seca, his wife Amparo and their three sons, Mercedes, Jean and Pancho. Pancho had died in February 1903 and the family had left the house soon after. Near to the house was a chemist shop just as Eduardo had claimed. By the time that Eduardo and his parents visited Rue Campanario, at some unspecified date in 1907, the Seca family had left Havana.

From the dates contained in Stevenson's report of this case (38) it is evident that Eduardo must have been conceived within a few months of the death of Pancho. In this respect it resembles the Alexandrina Samona case where the Alexandrina II was born the in same year that Alexandrina I had died.

Assessment of the case of Eduardo Esplugus-Cabrera

The only fact that Eduardo gave about his putative previous life that was incorrect was his father's first name. At face value this seems an unlikely error but, of course, it is not uncommon for individuals to have a nickname within their family that is different to their public name. A more sinister interpretation would be that the family fabricated the story and coached their four year old son to make the claims that he did. On this hypothesis Eduardo's memory failed him on this single fact. An alternative trivial explanation would be that a third party, unknown to the parents gave the child the facts that he subsequently 'recalled'. Given that Eduardo was only four years old at the time this explanation seems highly improbable.

Finally, one must consider the possibility that Eduardo acquired his knowledge of Pancho's life and death by paranormal means rather than by recollection of a previous life. As in the cases already described the behaviour of Eduardo does not resemble his possession by Pancho. Instead, he claims that in his present life he is Eduardo but that in a *previous* life he had been Pancho.

This same characteristic of Eduardo's behaviour does not favour an explanation based either on retrocognition, whereby one experiences an event which actually took place in the past or on precognition in which the percipient becomes aware of an event in advance of its actual occurrence; in this case the results of the visit of Eduardo and his parents to Rue Campanario. Eduardo did not report having such experiences but simply claims that he remembers a past life. In principle one could suggest that Eduardo had actually acquired his knowledge of Pancho's life by retrocognition when he was very young but that he had forgotten this source of his information by the time he was four.

Additional cases

In 1974 Ian Stevenson, published *Twenty Cases Suggestive of Reincarnation* (39). The book represented a collection of data obtained by interviewing children, their relatives and acquaintances in India (seven cases), Ceylon (now Sri Lanka) (3 cases), Brazil (2 cases), SouthEastern Alaska (7 cases), Lebanon (1 case). The Alaskan cases were all from the indigenous Tlingit Indians.

According to Stevenson's findings:

93

So far, the history of cases suggestive of reincarnation in India (and elsewhere) follow an almost conventional pattern. The case usually starts when a small child of two to four years of age begins talking to his parents or siblings of a life he led in another time and place. The child usually feels a considerable pull back toward the events of that life and he frequently importunes his parents to let him return to the community where he claims that he formally lived. If the child makes enough particular statements about the previous life, the parents (usually reluctantly) begin inquiries about their accuracy.

A critical assessment of Stevenson's book was made by Ian Wilson and was published in two books of his own (24, 28). Wilson noted that the cases reported by Stevenson were similar within any one culture but differed from one culture to another. The Tlingit Indians of Alaska believe that reincarnation takes place within the same family group and the cases that they report comply with this belief. In contrast cases reported among Hindus involved reincarnations into different families. While these cultural differences may be considered to raise doubts about the validity of the claims of the two ethnic groups we cannot decide *a priori* what characteristics reincarnation should have. In principle children might be reincarnated in accordance with the cultural beliefs of the society they come from and into which they return.

In further casting doubt on the value of Stevenson's data Wilson made much of the fact that in the Hindu cases it was often, but not always, claimed that the life in a previous incarnation had been spent in a higher caste family that the one in which the child was 'reborn'. He points out that there are certain advantages for a child in India to claim to have belonged to a higher caste and to have had more wealthy parents in a previous life. This criticism cannot be regarded as being one of substance. In a caste-conscious society a child is unlikely to claim that he, or she, was originally from a lower caste family and the child's parents would be expected to discourage any child from holding such a view. Consequently, social pressures may readily account for the bias in the data to which Wilson draws attention and through which he suggest the cases are fraudulent.

Stevenson's book contains a wealth of detail concerning each childhood case. However, despite his diligence in accumulating

94

data Stevenson takes pains to point out that his findings are only *suggestive* of reincarnation. As the discussion of the earlier cases that I have described above illustrates, the intrinsic difficulty is in rigorously excluding alternative explanations for the knowledge that the children have of their putative past lives.

Summary of evidence for reincarnation

Research into the paranormal is difficult for the reasons mentioned earlier. In spontaneous cases repeat experiments are not possible and in many cases the same observation may be accounted for by more than one paranormal phenomenon. Similarly, it is difficult, if not impossible to consider what types of experimental control would be considered applicable or even possible. Despite these difficulties no one considering objectively the evidence for telepathy, seeing-at-a-distance or precognition (see below) would dispute the validity of these phenomena even if one took into account spontaneous cases only.

With reincarnation the situation is even more difficult. From the published reports one can find both evidence for and evidence against it. There seems no doubt that some of the cases purported to suggest reincarnation are flawed. The Jane Evans case described above is one such example. Here cryptomnesia provided Jane with a convincing account of a past life. Such cases are misleadingly convincing because the hypnotised subject is not engaged in conscious fabrication and subsequently seems as astonished as anyone of the account they have given while hypnotised. While there seems to be no positive evidence in favour of the suggestion, I do feel that the Mary Baker case may fall into the same category as the Jane Evans one.

The Bridey Murphy case illustrates one other difficulty with reincarnation research. No orthodox Christian can accept reincarnation and with this case it appears that fundamentalist Christians tried, using false statements, to discredit it. Given that a newspaper was enthusiastically willing to publish this false evidence and at least one member of its staff ready to help in its fabrication one can see how those opposed to the existence of reincarnation could dismiss the Bridey Murphy case. However, the detailed and objective examination of the case by Ducasse (see above) would suggest that those who wished to discredit its

95

supposed support for the idea of reincarnation would have done better to have challenged its interpretation rather than its facts.

With cases involving the recollection of past lives by children one avoids the pitfalls of hypnosis-induced regression. However, I have already described the near impossibility of rigorously excluding alternative explanations to reincarnation for the childhood data. Becker produces reasonable arguments against super ESP hypotheses (37b) but the most objective comment that I feel is justified is that the best cases strongly support the concept of reincarnation, but that support does not mean proof.

On the issue of fraud one can only say that this is an ad hoc hypothesis – naturally one cannot rule out fraud in any one individual case but to dismiss all childhood data for reincarnation (27, 34, 38, 39) as fraudulent sounds a little like the argument that one encounters for dismissing all other paranormal phenomena.

Despite the innate difficulties in establishing the existence of reincarnation from the testimonies of those who claim to have lived before I do believe that from some previous existence we bring with us at birth a distillation of the experiences we have had before we were born. Whether such pre-birth experiences are obtained on this earth or elsewhere I have no strong view. It is a notable feature of all the childhood cases of reincarnation that I have found in the literature concern previous lives that were cut short by disease or violence. In no case does a child claim to recollect a previous life that ran to a full natural span. One can only speculate on the explanation. I am inclined to accept the evidence that those who die in childhood, and who therefore do not have a normal lifespan, are soon reborn on this earth, possibly into the same community in which they died early. Whether those who die in old age are reincarnated but have no recollection of their previous life, is a tenable but un-testable hypothesis. In the childhood cases reincarnation seems to follow soon after death but if this period is more lengthy then possibly the previous life memory fades. Certainly, if recollection of a previous life is an invariable feature of reincarnation then most of us are not reincarnated. Alternatively, if we have experienced former lives but have no recollection of them one may ask in what way can they bring about spiritual growth. I suspect that for the Hindu the answer might be couched in terms of the loss of something, rather than in the gain of something else. If that which prevents us from realising our final destiny is illusion and ignorance, then to lose these imperfections would help the soul to attain its ultimate goal.

A man acts according to the desires to which he clings. After death he goes into the next world bearing in his mind the subtle impressions of his deeds; and after reaping there the harvest of his deeds, he returns again to this world of action. Thus he who desires continues subject to rebirth. But he in whom desire is stilled suffers no rebirth. After death, having attained to the highest, desiring only Self, he goes to no other world. Realising Brahman, he becomes Brahman. Brihadaranyaka. The Upanishads (40)

Precognition and Retrocognition

Historically man has developed several methods of divination: the earliest known Chinese writing has been found inscribed on the 'oracle' bones of pig, ox and sheep dating from the 19th to 11th centuries BC. The patterns of cracks induced by the application of hot brands were interpreted as divine guidance from royal ancestors. In Judaism the prophetic value of dreams are first recorded in the Book of Genesis, c.13th century BC and in classical times the Oracle at Delphi was consulted, on payment of a fee, by all those seeking knowledge of the future from the Pythia, the priestess to whom the powers of prophecy were accredited. In more primitive cultures particular individuals, shamans, were also believed to have the ability to foretell the future. As we have already noted, the development of astronomy in ancient Babylon was accompanied by a belief in the predictive properties of the constellations. Remarkably astrology still has a significant following.

Only in relatively recent times has there been a scientific evaluation of the validity of the concept of precognition. An excellent account is given by A E Roy in his chapter, *Precognition – a Sort of Radar,* (41). Here he says:

.. if one reads through the Proceedings and Journals of the British and American Societies for Psychical research, one may come to a certain definite opinion that precognition (paranormally acquired information of the future) and retrocognition (paranormally acquired information of the past) are established facts from the weight of evidence.

Needless to say, in principle the paranormal nature of precognition should be more readily substantiated than that of retrocognition because only in the former can it be excluded that non-paranormal sources of information are involved. For this reason retrocognition will not be discussed further here even though the evidence for such a phenomenon is good. Roy gives a few examples of precognition that give him grounds for the confidence of his assertion. The evidence, as with many other paranormal phenomena derives both from spontaneous cases and laboratory studies. The spontaneous cases are the more striking but the laboratory ones lend themselves to statistical analysis and to the determination of the factors that affect the phenomenon.

Some examples:

On 21st October 1966 at 9:15am part of a coal tip, made unstable by heavy rain, slipped down to engulf part of the Welsh village of Aberfan. One hundred and forty-four people died including one hundred and twenty-eight children at the Pantglas junior school. A psychiatrist, JC Barker, visited Aberfan the day after the disaster and was appalled by what he saw. He had a long-term interest in the paranormal and he decided to make an appeal through the media for individuals who had any premonition of the disaster, to contact him. He had 76 replies of which he found 24 where accounts of the premonitions were given to reliable independent witnesses before the disaster took place (35). A brief description of two of these cases follows.

The first report was prepared by the Rev. Glannan Jones and signed by both of the parents of the child involved. A fortnight before the disaster a 10 year old pupil at Pantglas school said to her mother 'Mummy, I am not afraid to die.' Her mother, no doubt to divert her from such apparently inappropriate thoughts asked her if she wanted a lollipop. 'No', said the child, 'but I shall be with Peter and June.' The day before the disaster she insisted on telling her mother of her dream of the previous night. 'I dreamt I went to school and there was no school there. Something black had come down over it'. The next day she went happily off to school. In the communal grave she was buried (at the parents' request) with her school friends, Peter on one side and June on the other.

In a second case a Mrs Constance Milder, of Plymouth, 'saw' an old school house in a valley, then a Welsh miner, then an avalanche of coal hurtling down a mountainside. She then saw a terrified and grief stricken little boy and with him one of the rescuers who was wearing an unusual peaked cap. Shortly afterwards the BBC transmitted a programme about the disaster and Mrs Milder recognised the little boy of her vision, by his long fringe and the rescuer who was with him wearing his peaked cap. Mrs Milder reported her vision to six witnesses on the day before the disaster and to her neighbour 45 minutes before it happened. All the witnesses confirmed Mrs Milder's report in writing.

Barker noted that many of the other cases could be classified into a few different groups. Some were visions of the event, or part of it, others were dreams, sometimes so terrifying that the dreamer woke screaming and some were simply feelings of acute anxiety and foreboding.

Experimental investigations of precognition

Some of the earlier experiments to seek for evidence for precognition were the well known ones of Professor J.B. Rhine (43). In these experiments studies were made of to what extent an individual could predict the sequence of a pack of cards which were subject to a randomisation procedure *after* the prediction had been recorded. In other and more recent experiments measurement by H.Schmidt have been made of the ability of a subject to predict an event whose occurrence was determined by the radioactivity of a strontium 90 source (44). These experiments have become increasingly sophisticated with the realisation that, given the evidence for psychokinesis (PK), the individual taking part in the test may, in principle at least, achieve a better than chance score by mentally influencing the randomisation process itself. Ingenious steps have been taken to avoid this possibility, for example by incorporating the numerical value of the environmental temperature on the day into the randomisation procedure. All of these experiments produced statistically significant results. For example, the odds against chance being responsible for the results of Schmidt's experiments was of the order 10^{10} to 1.

Implications of precognition

At first sight precognition seems to present us with two paradoxes. If the future is predictable in advance how can the concept of free will be sustained and, at a more practical level, how can detailed knowledge of an event be obtained days before it has happened?

Following the Aberfan disaster and the demonstration that a number of individuals had premonitions of the event a 'British Premonitions Bureau' was set up in 1967. In its first year over 500 premonitions were received. The chapter by A E Roy (41) gives details of two of these; one relating to a lorry with an exceptionally heavy load and the other to an aeroplane crash in which children were involved and where the tail fin of the plane figured strongly. Within one week of the first premonition a crash occurred at a level crossing between an express train and a low loader carrying a giant transformer. Twelve people were killed. Similarly, within 5 weeks of the second premonition a British Midland Airways Argonaut crashed with the deaths of almost all the passengers, some of whom were children. Significantly, photographs of the tail fin of the aircraft, which was the only part recognisable after the crash, appeared in many newspaper and TV reports.

It seems reasonable to claim that the two premonitions described were precognitions of the two disasters mentioned. However, it is notable that in neither case were the premonitions sufficiently specific to allow steps to be taken to avoid the disasters to which they relate. Unfortunately, details are not given of the other 500 or so premonitions but one must suppose that they were no more successful in preventing disasters than the ones described. Significantly, the British Premonitions Bureau closed a few years after it was set up because of its limited success. Without more information one cannot make any firm conclusion but until there is evidence to the contrary it seems that a precognition will not enable a change in the future to be brought about by the premonition itself, either because premonitions lack the essential detail that makes it possible for human action to prevent a disaster or that because the nature of the disaster is such that it is beyond human control. There is, of course, a logical inconsistency in supposing that the premonition of an event can prevent it happening since then the premonition of the event occurring would be false. The premonitions that do occur are not conditional, that is, they are not of the form '*if A happens then B will occur.*' For example the Aberfan disaster was not preceded by a premonition that, *if a coal tip were to be placed at Aberfan, then there would be a disaster.* Instead the premonitions were such that they predicted a disaster that did happen. All the pre-conditions required were in place by the time that it occurred.

However, the apparent inevitability of such events does not necessarily imply that free will is merely an illusion. Whereas there seems to be no evidence that premonitions can prevent the occurrence of an event, they can apparently influence the outcome of a disaster for the potential victims. In 1890, at the Marfa colliery at Port Talbot, South Wales, an explosion killed all the 87 miners in the pit. The reason that the death toll was not larger was that more than half the miners stayed away from work on that day because of a widespread feeling of anxiety and foreboding that pervaded the town on the morning of the disaster. It would appear that, whereas the pit explosion was unavoidable by any human means, the miners of the Marfa colliery were free to choose whether they went to work that day or not.

With regard to the question of how one can acquire information of an event before it happens, the straightforward answer is that we do not know. The fact of precognition would seem to imply either that our commonsense view of time is inadequate, or that we can sometimes acquire by paranormal means knowledge of events that are inevitably going to occur. We have already noted that 'commonsense' is a very poor guide to what may be. However, the problem posed by precognition is but one example of how paranormal phenomena challenge our everyday view of reality.

Free Will

The brief discussion of free will in the previous section is much more limited than this complex topic merits. There is a vast literature on the subject of free will but, in keeping with the aims of this book I shall give only my own views and leave the rest to the philosophers who have continued to discus the subject since Aristotle.

From the physical scientist's point of view the mere existence of free will constitutes a problem. When the Mechanical Philosophy held sway in France Voltaire remarked

> *'it would be very singular that all nature, all the planets, should obey eternal laws, and there should be a little animal, five feet high, who, in contempt of these laws, could act as he pleased, solely according to his caprice.'* (5f)

101

With the downfall of the Mechanical Philosophy and the introduction, via the quantum theory, of uncertainty, it might be thought that Voltaire's comment had lost its weight. However, subjectively we do not experience free will as a manifestation of uncertainty. At least I have the illusion that I have choice in what I write in the next sentence. Indeed, it is not possible to conceive that I am able to write anything coherent if all my decision-making was an accumulation of a series of events determined only by probable outcomes. However, whether or not I truly have free will is not settled by dismissing the argument that quantum uncertainty enables us to escape determinism. A psychologist may argue that all my decision-making (and, therefore, his) is not truly an expression of free will but only responses to present and past stimuli of which I may not directly be aware. This is essentially Voltaire's proposition again and it can be seen to carry some weight. For example, whether or not I decide to make a pilgrimage to Mecca or to Rome will be strongly influenced by whether or not I have been raised as a Muslim or as a Catholic. Further, one of the features that defines one's character is the type of choice that one makes in a given circumstance. A cautious man is likely to make a less risky choice than a bold or impulsive one. If we were entirely predictable in this way then we have no free will and our discussion should, instead be centred on identifying those factors that determine our temperament. The effect that experience and environment has on our decision-making cannot be disputed but it has important social implications. Individuals who have been in care as a child or who have educational difficulties or have suffered unemployment are much more likely to end up in prison than those of us who have not.

There will be those who argue that these characteristics of prisoners are no more that the expression of genetic traits inherited from their (often) dysfunctional parents. Secular society as a whole does not accept this view in that it holds an individual responsible for his/her actions; more significantly, all the major religions seem to agree. However, this comment requires some modification, at least with respect to Hinduism as the following quote makes clear.

The will as conceived by the Upanishads, and other Indian scriptures, has in it an element of complete freedom, a power sufficient to enable a man to act in direct opposition to the spontaneous tendency of his accumulated character- and therefore to control his future.

102

An element of complete freedom – observe. The will, to an indetermiate extent, is itself caught up in the hard chain of cause and effect, is itself formed and modified by deeds. The outward act you perform today, the thought you think, qualify your will of the next moment, your will of tomorrow. They make it better, or they make it worse; still in the next moment, or tomorrow, there still remains that particle of ineluctable liberty that permits you to remake your life.

The Spiritual Heritage of India. (23b)

This is a much more attractive concept than that of determinism; it is at the same time, challenging and hopeful and it contains enough of determinism for society to understand those who transgress its laws.

There is a second characteristic of human behaviour that has implications for the conclusions that we draw about free will. The most cursory examination of human history illustrates that groups of people often behave collectively in a very different way to that when they act as individuals. Society actually condones, or even glorifies this difference. Thus it is universally considered a crime if one person kills an innocent individual but murder on an international scale, as in war, is generally accepted and even lauded. I find it difficult to account for this difference in the value put on human life without arguing that warfare is essentially a manifestation of tribalism. One may look for parallels in the behaviour of other primates. For example, baboons are social animals that live in troops. A troop will defend its own living area against other baboon troops by displaying signs of aggression. However, an unprofitable level of aggression between different troops is rare, presumably because it is instinctively limited. It seems that such confrontation does not lead to bloodshed because the less powerful troop will withdraw. With humankind this instinctive restraint has disappeared and tribal identity in war is generally so strong that the most horrific acts of violence may be committed in order to defend a nation's integrity or even to oppose a perceived, but as yet unrealised threat to it. Indeed, self defence has not, in the past at least, provided the sole reason for acts of national aggression-man has a long history of imperialism, a type of behaviour not found in the animal kingdom to my knowledge.

It is curious that humankind, which has no threat to its survival from other species, has developed its own and thereby generated

103

its own pressure to evolve. What is clear is that now that at least seven nations possess nuclear weapons, and that each of these is twenty times or more powerful than the bomb that destroyed Hiroshima, the world must quickly find another way of settling its tribal disputes other than by total war. Currently mankind is in a transitional period where he has evolved past the stage where instinct limits the violence that a species inflicts upon itself, but he has not yet reached one where wisdom limits the destructive power that is a direct product of his intellect. I am optimistic that he will, if only because I do not believe that a billion years of biological evolution on this planet will lead to a self-inflicted termination of its most evolved species. In this context it is worth noting that civilisation has existed for only about 500 generations.

The Contribution of Science to Man's Spirituality

Earlier in this book I have set out my reasons for questioning the ability of science to give a comprehensive explanation of the physical world. However, to leave the issue there would be to give a totally distorted impression of my own view of the contribution of science to Man's spirituality. Scientific endeavour has contributed to human experience beyond anything that would have been anticipated even a century ago. However, it has not diminished the mystery; rather it has expanded it.

The most beautiful and most profound emotion we can experience is the sensation of the mystical. It is the sower of all true science. He to whom this emotion is a stranger, who can no longer wonder and stand rapt in awe, is as good as dead.

Albert Einstein

The scientist does not study nature because it is useful, he studies it because he delights in it because it is beautiful. If nature were not beautiful, it would not be worth knowing, and if nature were not worth knowing, life would not be worth living.

Henri Poincaré

The geocentric model of the Universe was attractive to the Church in Galileo's day; as man was made in the image of God it was appropriate that he should be at the centre of Creation. The picture today looks very different. The earth is a planet that orbits

104

one star in the Milky Way galaxy. The galaxy contains about 100 billion stars, about twenty stars for each person on earth. The galaxy is of such a size that light, travelling at 186,000 miles per second, takes 80,000 years to cross it. Furthermore, there are about 100 billion galaxies in the Universe that is about 12 billion light years in size. Recent observations indicate that stars with planets orbiting them are likely to be quite common in the Universe. Unless one wishes to regard all but a tiny part of the Universe as redundant as far as life is concerned, we conclude that mankind, whose written history dates back only 5000 years (i.e. only one millionth as long as the age of the solar system), is most unlikely to be the most highly evolved life form in the Universe. It seems that there is little room for fundamentalism, be it of the religious or scientific kind.

Science has revealed a Universe that is unimaginably vast. Observations made as deep into space as our telescopes can see, indicate that the same physical laws pertain throughout. While much is chaotic, yet even the chaos obeys statistical laws. The contribution that science has made to religion is not to provide an explanation for our existence, but rather to demonstrate that we are part of a creation that dwarfs our ability to comprehend it and that makes it the more incredible that we exist at all.

But the revelations of science, even when they go far beyond man's power of direct perception, give him the purest feeling of disinterested delight and a supersensual background to his world. Science offers us the mystical knowledge of matter which often passes the range of our imagination. Rabindranath Tagore

The Western Attitude to Death

Whereas for many it seems self evident that we are more than that which a materialistic view of the world would allow, we do live in a materialistic age in which the reassurances of religion have given way to an almost insatiable consumerism. This seeking for more material goods is an unconscious attempt to divert our attention from what we have lost. For others narcotics or alcohol provide a means of escape from an apparently meaningless existence.

Paradoxically, in view of what I have just written about the contribution of science to religion, to some degree at least the successes of science in apparently making the physical world intelligible is responsible for the growth of materialism. One further sad consequence of this growth is that for many death, which no level of consumerism can conceal, has become the ultimate evil. As a result desperately sick people are kept alive by all technical means possible yielding a quality of life which it would be considered totally unethical to sustain in a domestic animal.

> *We have come to look upon life as a conflict with death – the intruding enemy, not the natural ending – in impotent quarrel with which we spend every stage of it. When time comes for youth to depart, we would hold it back by main force. When the fervour of desire slackens, we would revive it with fresh fuel of our own devising. When our sense organs weaken, we urge them to keep up their effort. Even when our grip has relaxed we are reluctant to give up possession. We are not trained to recognize the inevitable as natural, so cannot give up gracefully that which has to go, but needs must wait till it is snatched from us. The truth comes as a conqueror only because we have lost the art of receiving it as a guest.* Rabindranath Tagore (45a)

Of course, one cannot lay the ills of western culture at the door of science. As I have remarked already, the revelations of science, when viewed properly, serve only to enhance the sense of awe with which we see creation. Further, even at the material level few of us would relish a return to a pre-scientific era lifestyle.

The Implications of Paranormal Phenomena for Science.

One characteristic that is commonly demanded of any phenomenon that can be studied experimentally is that, provided the conditions under which the phenomenon is studied are well defined the results should be reproducible. No scientific 'fact' enters the corpus of scientific knowledge until it has been verified by scientists who are independent of those reporting the fact for the first time. This demand for reproducibility has served science well and prevented (usually) the survival of scientific myths. At first sight paranormal phenomena fail as scientific facts because generally they are not quantitatively reproducible. However, the dismissal of the validity of paranormal phenomena on the grounds of their irreproducibility is illogical because we do not know what constitutes a 'well-defined' system when we are dealing with things of the mind. In fact there is good evidence that an aggressive demand for the demonstration of a paranormal effect is almost a guarantee that it

106

will not occur. It seems that humility on the part of the enquirers is one of the conditions required for such effects to be observed. Needless to say, a need for humility is not commonly written into the methodology of scientific research.

Hans Driesch, in the Preface of his critical appraisal of research into the paranormal wrote (29),

> *People often regard themselves as very 'enlightened' when in fact they are the opposite, being merely dogmatically hidebound. They think they know what can happen and what can't. People have not even an idea what an exhaustive literature it (paranormal research) has.*

One might only add that since that statement was written in 1933 there has been a very considerable increase in the literature.

Religious Experiences

While the paranormal phenomena that I have briefly described refute materialistic dogma many people reject such dogma as a result of their own experience. We are aware that much of nature is inspiringly beautiful and one of the greatest gifts we have is a sense of beauty and things around us to which that sense of beauty can respond if we are open to it. I recall travelling west from Oxford one day on the top deck of a bus just as the sun was setting. The sky was a mass of different colours, from blazing gold and silver to red, orange, white and various shades of green, blue and indigo. The clouds sculptured these colours in fantastic ways that were a joy to witness. After a few moments I noticed that none of my fellow passengers were looking out of the windows but were apparently absorbed in reading papers, magazines and books.

Many of us can recall experiences like the one that I have described but sometimes a religious, or mystical experience can be qualitatively different being much more vivid and absorbing and often having a lifelong effect on the person experiencing it. I have already given a brief account of one of my own and they are far from rare. Here is one from the literature:

> *Finally let me describe an experience from a time many years later. It took place in a bleak and arid town in Northern India, with a few trees and little grass and an air of pervading squalor,*

during the hours of daylight. After a long period of worry and anxiety, I made a deliberate act of relaxation and there came upon me a sudden realization of the meaning of the words "God in whom we live and move and have our being. This resulted from a conscious surrender of all worries and responsibilities to God. I became, as it were, conscious of an all-pervading aether which seemed to flow through everything uniting me with the whole Universe. I became aware of being part of the miraculous process which kept the planets in their courses and of the mighty plan of the creation. I went out into the compound behind my flat, which looked out on to the railway. Beside the railway was a tin shack used by Muslim worshippers as a kind of improvised mosque, standing near a railway signal box. As I leant upon the gate in the dusk I suddenly felt again a sense of benediction and unity and security. I knew again that I was one with all created things, not only the stars and the stormy clouds above the horizon, which might have been part of a Dutch seascape, and with the trees with their brown velvet edges against the blue –green sky, but even the humble worshippers in the tin shack mosque, with a boy softly crooning an Indian love song as he wandered idly by me, with the little light above the heads of worshippers and the min-gling sound of approaching night. I felt a wonderful joy, a serene happiness, a sense that I belonged to all this, deep down in me, and that it all belonged to me: and there was nothing to fear, no need to feel anxiety about the future or the past: that one could trust life, and that everything was part of a kind of mysterious perfection and completeness. (46a)

And another from the same source, this time from an adult rec-ollecting a childhood experience.

It was a summer day and I was playing out back of the house, in an alley in the city where we lived. It was one of my happier days, when I had found playmates. A sudden storm came up and interrupted our play. I sat alone out there between garages behind the house waiting for it to end. It was near noon. The rain ended almost as soon as it came, and the sun shone hot and bright once more. All at once I felt as if I were seeing everything for the first time. The light seemed like gold, the smell of the wet foliage was like perfume, with the rainwater shining and running about in little rivulets, the humming and the buzzing of insects and bees was pleasant to my ears. Everywhere I looked there was beauty. In that dirty alley wherever there was a leaf or a blade of grass it sparkled. I was filled with a sense of great comfort and peace. Now I watched a beetle going about its business, and then a small garden spider, and I was glowing with warmth. It was as if all that was outside of me, I felt to be part of it. Then a thought came. It said, "See! Everything is alive, everything lives. That insect, it has life, the grass, the air even." And then I felt joy, and with joy, love and then a feeling of reverence. (46b)

Such experiences are not uncommon but the true number is probably concealed by the reluctance that people have to reveal that which is most personal and precious to them. Here is another example, this time from a different source.

About two years ago on an April morning I felt ill at ease and unhappy. Life was difficult and the burden of the war weighed upon me. I climbed the steep path at the entrance of one of our public parks and stood beneath some cherry trees that fringe the crest of the bank. A fresh wind blew dark clouds across the green-blue sky. The white blossom shone and glistened in the sunlight. As I stood relaxed and still, I had the illusion that I was enveloped in light. I had the feeling that the light and I were one. Time and space slipped from me. All awareness of details vanished. A sense of unity with the world entered into me. I was tranquillised and steadied by the beauty, the stability of nature. I do not suppose that I learnt anything that was new to me during this experience. But I believe I was taught something and that something happened in me. (47a)

A second from the same volume:
A sudden concentration of attention on a rainy August morning. Clusters of bright red berries, some wrinkled, some blemished, others perfect, hanging among green leaves. The experience could not have lasted more than a few seconds, but that was a moment out of time. I was caught up in what I saw: I became part of it: the berries, the leaves, the raindrops and I, we were all of a piece. A moment of beauty and harmony and meaning. A moment of understanding. (47b)

And another, from a different source.

In that time the consciousness of God's nearness came to me sometimes. I say God, to describe what is indescribable. A presence, I might say, yet that is too suggestive of personality, and the moments of which I speak did not hold the consciousness of personality, but something in myself made me feel part of something bigger than I, that was controlling. I felt myself one with the grass, the trees, birds, insects, everything in nature. I exulted in the mere fact of existence, of being part of it all- the drizzling rain, the shadows of the clouds, the tree trunks and so on. In the years following, such moments continued to come, but I wanted them constantly. I knew so well the satisfaction of losing self in a perception of supreme power and love, that I was unhappy because that perception was not constant. (18b)

Finally, two further ones. Both appeared on BBC Television but I do not know the names of those involved and I write only from my own recollection of what the individuals said.

In one of the Southern States of the USA a young Negro was sent to prison. He was the son of a prostitute who had taken no interest in his well-being and he spent much of his childhood in a wooden shack on the edge of his home town. His drift into crime was almost inevitable. In prison he was racially provoked by a white prisoner and the two came to blows. As punishment the Negro was given solitary confinement in a cell that was completely dark and that had no furniture but a concrete plinth that was to serve as a bed. He sat on the plinth and soon began to notice that his feet were wet. He discovered that they were wet with his own tears. At once the cell was filled with a bright light and he felt an overpowering sensation of being loved.

This experience changed his life. He became a gentle, law-abiding and happily married citizen with an unshakeable faith in the love of God. He repeatedly went back to prison but now to talk to other prisoners to convince them that they too were much loved.

A second example of a life-changing religious experience concerned a drug addict in the UK who, in deep despair, began to contemplate suicide. His story was broadcast in one of the BBC 'Songs of Praise' programmes. As with the Negro in the previous account a religious experience at this time of personal crisis had a permanent life-changing effect on him. He too felt that there was some power that loved him deeply and that had a purpose for him. He gave up drugs and looked around for ways that could help other addicts whom he had known. He realised that in the neighbourhood there were many elderly people who needed the assistance of able-bodied young people to mow their lawns, cultivate their gardens and do the many other tasks that age makes difficult. The ex-drug addict brought these two groups of people together. The elderly lost their fear of the addicts and had the help that they needed while the drug addicts gained the affection of those that they helped and also their own self-respect.

Many religious experiences are not as dramatic as these but they are probably much more common. The Religious Experience Research Centre, founded by Sir Alister Hardy at Oxford and now at the University of Wales at Lampeter has over 5000 first-person accounts of religious experiences of various kinds. Many, but by no means all concern personal crises such as those associated with a period of anxiety or with the death of a loved one. The experience that I had when my son was dying was not atypical but in some at least experiences have been of considerably longer duration than was mine. As some of the examples that I have quoted make clear, in many cases the religious experience is a feeling of being greatly loved and often there is a feeling that all things are really one indivisible whole – a whole that includes the person having the experience. Almost always there is a feeling of joy during the experience.

A cynic might suggest that religious experiences, at least at times of stress, are no more than hallucinations to protect the psyche from a painful emotion. To my mind this view is rendered unlikely by the fact that such an experience often has a life-long effect and in many cases a religious experience can occur in unstressful circumstances. Certainly, those who have had a religious experience do not question its validity and it remains a most precious possession. The language used by the adult recollecting her childhood in one of the above extracts illustrated just how vivid is the memory recalled.

In his Introduction to his Ely Lectures delivered at Union Theological Seminary, New York the American Quaker Rufus Jones writes

The main attack in recent years on the validity of mysticism as a religious experience is the characteristic attack of the psychol-

ogist. He insists that the experience is purely subjective and consequently lacks objective reference to any reality beyond the individual who has the experience. He brackets drug-intoxications, the spells of medicine men, hypnotic states, and hysterical trances with the exalted experiences of God which have come to mystics, and then proceeds to show that they are one and all alike "such stuff as dreams are made of" – in short, purely subjective creations...... There is no good ground, or sound basis, however, for limiting mystical experience to any such contracted field. The same psychological method applied to any form of sense experience in the same limited way would equally deprive it of its objective reality. There is no way of proving that our unmediated sensations of colour, of sound, of odour, of taste, of roughness or smoothness or hardness, stand for objective realities precisely like our subjective experience of them. (48)

One might criticise this statement on the grounds that, whereas religious experience is essentially personal, the world of common perception is shared by all. However, individuals who are colour blind do not convince the rest of us that our distinction between red and green is *such stuff as dreams are made of.* If most people had religious experiences it would be the minority who did not have them who would be regarded as lacking in perception. To rule against religious experience is to deny our ability to see farther than our five senses allow.

William James, in his book The Varieties of Religious Experience, already cited above, is rather more forthright:

...so long as we deal with the cosmic and the general, we deal only with the symbols of reality, but as soon as we deal with private and personal phenomena as such, we deal with realities in the completest sense of the term. That unsharable feeling which each of us has of the pinch of his individual destiny as he privately feels it rolling out on fortune's wheel may be disparaged for its egotism, may be sneered at as unscientific, but it is the one thing that fills up the measure of our concrete actuality, and any would-be existent that should lack such a feeling, or its analogue, would be a piece of reality only half made up. (18c)

The claim for the validity of religious experience has been made equally emotively by William Dampier. From his choice of words it seems abundantly clear that he is speaking of an experience of his own.

> *Science must admit the psychological validity of religious experience. The mystical and direct apprehension of God is clearly to some men as real as their perception of the external world. It is this sense of the communion with the Divine, and the awe and worship which it evokes, that constitutes religion – to most a vision seen only at moments of exaltation, but to the Saints an experience as normal, all-pervading and perpetual as the breath of life. It is not necessary, indeed it is impossible, to define what is meant by God; those who know him will want no definition.* (5b)

Near Death Experiences

Near-death experiences are not new and have been reported throughout the ages from almost all cultures and religious traditions. However, with the development of modern techniques of resuscitation the frequency of near-death experiences has increased substantially and since these often occur in a hospital environment an objective assessment of the medical condition of an individual having such an experience can now be made. In 1975 Raymond Moody published the first study of near-death experiences (NDEs) of hospital patients (49) and several studies since then have confirmed and expanded his findings (see for example (50, 51).

It is sometimes possible to restore life to those who, by the objective criteria of an absence of heartbeat and respiration and with fixed, dilated pupils are technically dead. After resuscitation approximately 10% of such individuals report having had an experience during this near-death episode that they are able to recall on regaining consciousness. The various accounts show many features in common. The patient may have a sensation of having left the body and of looking down from above at the resuscitation attempts taking place. They sometimes give accurate details of what they have observed during this out-of-body experience though these observations would have not been possible from the vantage point of the bed on which their unconscious body lay.

In addition they report meeting deceased friends or relatives, who appear in their prime rather than in the state that they were when they died. In one case a patient reported meeting a relative who, unbeknown to them, had died a short time before their own near-death experience. Sometimes they report meeting religious figures familiar to them from their own faith tradition. They may experience a review of their past life, in the presence of a compassionate being who is full of love for them.

To illustrate the points about the near-death-experience made in the above introduction to this topic the following account of a specific case will be given. It is an abridged part of the contribution of Professor Ring to the book 'Thinking Beyond the Brain' (51).

'...one of our respondents, a forty-five year old woman named Vicki, told us of the time she found herself floating above her body in the emergency room of a hospital following an automobile accident. She was aware of being up near the ceiling watching a male doctor and a female nurse working on her body, which she viewed from her elevated position. Vicki has a clear recollection of how she came to the realisation that this was her own body below her.'

I knew it was me...I was pretty thin then I was quite tall and thin at that point. And I recognised at first that it was a body, but I did not know that it was mine initially. Then I perceived that I was up on the ceiling and I thought, 'Well, that's kind of weird. What am I doing up here?' I thought, 'Well, this must be me. Am I dead?...' I just briefly saw this body, and...I knew that it was mine because I wasn't in mine.

In addition, she was able to note certain further identifying features indicating that the body she was observing was certainly her own:

I think I was wearing the plain gold band on my right ring finger and my father's wedding ring next to it. But my wedding ring I definitely saw...That was the one I noticed the most because its most unusual. It has orange blossoms on the corners of it.

Professor Ring goes on to say: 'As twenty-five years of research into NDEs has shown, such reports of visual out-of-body perception are by no means rare among persons coming close to death, but are indeed so common that most readers of this article will already be familiar with them. Yet there is something extremely remarkable and provocative about Vicki's recollection of these visual impressions, as her subsequent comment implies.

This was,' she said, *'the only time I could ever relate to seeing and to what light was, because I experienced it.*

In short, what is astonishing about Vicki's account is that she had never previously been able to see at all. She was born blind, her optic nerve having been completely destroyed at birth because of an excess of oxygen she received in the incubator. Yet, she appears to have seen during her NDE.

She then told us that following her out-of-body episode, which was very fast and fleeting, she found herself going up through the ceilings of the hospital until she was above the roof of the building itself, during which time she had a brief panoramic view of her surroundings. She felt very exhilarated during this ascension and enjoyed tremendously the freedom of movement she was experiencing. She also began to hear sublimely beautiful and exquisitely harmonious music akin to wind chimes.

With scarcely a noticeable transition, she discovered she had been sucked in head first into a tube and felt she was being pulled up into it. The enclosure itself was dark, Vicki said, yet she was aware she was moving towards light. As she reached the opening of the tube, the music she had heard earlier seemed to be transformed into hymns and she then 'rolled out' to find herself lying on grass.

She was surrounded by trees and flowers and a vast number of people. She was in a place of tremendous light, and the light, Vicki said, was something that you could feel as a well as see. Even the people she saw were bright. 'Everybody there was made of light. And I was made of light.' What the light conveyed was love. 'There was love everywhere. It was like love came from the grass, love came from the birds, love came from the trees.'

Vicki then became aware of specific persons she knew in life who are welcoming her to this place. There are five of them. Debbie and Diane were Vicki's blind schoolmates who had died years before, at age 11 and 6, respectively. In life, they had both been profoundly retarded as well as blind, but here they appeared bright and beautiful, healthy and vitally alive. And no longer children, but as Vicki phrased it, in their prime. In addition, Vicki reports seeing two of her childhood caretakers, a couple named Mr and Mrs Silk, both of whom had also previously died. Finally, there was Vicki's grandmother – who had essentially raised Vicki and who had died just two years before this incident. In these encounters, no actual words were exchanged, Vicki says, but only feelings – feelings of love and welcome.

In the midst of this rapture, Vicki is suddenly overcome with a sense of total knowledge:

> *I had a feeling like I knew everything…and everything made sense. I just knew that this was where…this place was where I would find the answers to all the questions about life, and about the planets, and about God, and about everything…It's like the place is the knowing……*

As these revelations are unfolding, Vicki notices that next to her is a figure whose radiance is far greater than the illumination of any of the persons she has so far encountered. Immediately she recognises this being to be Jesus. He greets her tenderly, while she conveys her excitement to him about her newfound omniscience and her joy at being there with him.

Vicki's NDE comes to an end when the radiant being tells her '*But you can't stay here now. It's not your time to be here yet and you have to go back.*'

Naturally, Vicki is very reluctant to do so but the being reassures her that she will come back, but for now, she '*has to go back and learn and teach more about loving and forgiving*'. She then learns that she also needs to go back to have her children. With that, Vicki, who was then childless but who 'desperately wanted' children (and who has since given birth to three) becomes almost eager to return.

However, before Vicki can leave, the being says to her, in these exact words, '*But first, watch this.*'

And what Vicki then sees is '*everything from my birth*' in a complete panoramic review of her life, and as she watches, the being gently comments to help her understand the significance of her actions and their repercussions.

The last thing Vicki remembers, once the life review has been completed, are the words, *'You have to leave now.'* The return is sudden rather than a reversal of her outward journey.

Professor Ring's research indicated the experience of seeing during NDE is common among blind people so that Vicki's experience is by no means unique. From this account it is evident that the NDE of blind people is essentially the same as that of sighted individuals.

Conclusion

In the foregoing I have described rather briefly those experiences, either my own or those of others with whom I feel in harmony, upon which I have formulated my beliefs. While nothing that I can say can be original, it is my personal view and it must be the foundation of my attempts to interpret the world as I experience it. To make any such interpretation is ambitious and it may be considered foolish to make the attempt at all. However, not to attempt a synthesis, however tentative and certainly incalculably incomplete, seems to imply that we can learn nothing of value from our living.

First, there is an abundance of evidence to enable us to completely dismiss the model of the Universe that defines reality as that which is perceived solely by the five senses. Although we live in an age in which materialism has threatened to reduce us to an assembly of highly complex biochemical systems in which only quantum physics prevents us from being totally predictable and where free will has no place, most of us reject such a concept. It is notable that we have no understanding of consciousness and can therefore have no scientific description of what we are. Earlier in this book I have emphasised just how incomplete are scientific explanations, even for the world of our shared perceptions. For our unshared perceptions, those personal experiences and subjective feelings and emotions that contribute in such a significant measure to our individuality, no purely material, mechanistic analysis can be acceptable. In short, we are unwilling to consider ourselves solely as beings suitable for examination by our own microscopes. If we needed any further, more detached reasons for rejecting a materialistic view of reality there is the compelling evidence for a wide range of paranormal phenomena, which reveals that we are even more complex than modern science has found us to be. Naturally, this conclusion would have been regarded as self evident by the mystics of all of the religions of the world but mysticism does not flourish in the sterile soil of materialism.

If one rejects materialism in favour of religion the innocent enquirer might ask, which of the vast number that mankind has developed is the 'correct' one? The problem is not entirely trivial since there are almost innumerable world religions, and while some have relatively few devotees even the major religions have undergone schisms since they were first founded. Some of the sectarian violence that has arisen as a consequence of these schisms has violated the very essence of the religious beliefs of the conflicting sects.

What we seek is a belief that puts aside these religious and sectarian differences and instead that recognises those features of our existence that unite us. Such a belief cannot depend on the adherence to any specific religious dogma. This is not simply because dogma is the foundation of religious fundamentalism which so often in the past has provided the grounds for religious persecution, but because the acceptance of dogma imposes an artificial boundary that specifies in advance what is true and prevents us from seeking truth wherever it may be found.

Do not depend on doctrines, do not depend on dogmas, or sects, or churches, or temples; they count for little compared with the essence of existence in man, which is divine;

Ramakrishna. (23c)

I believe that we will be wise to seek truth as close to the source of spiritual inspiration as is possible. It will be noted that the accounts of contemporary religious experiences that I have described above share common features. There is a sense of joy, of a unity of creation and a feeling of being greatly loved. The source of this love is not sharply defined though the word 'God' is used by some. These characteristics of religious experiences are also found in the cases of Near Death Experiences that I have also described. I believe that all of these have intrinsic validity. We do not understand how we have come into being but we are part of a great whole, we are inestimably valuable, we are greatly loved and death is but a change into a new manifestation of life. Not

118

surprisingly all the major religions, stripped of their dogma assert just the same truths, but what I find particularly valuable about the contemporary religious experiences of the sort that I have reproduced here is their vividness and accessibility.

> *The humble, meek, merciful, just, pious, and devout souls are everywhere of one religion; and when death has taken off the mask they will know one another, though divers liveries they wear here makes them strangers.* William Penn

It is notable that these truths are found, not by reason, but by experience. While it is true that not all of us have profound religious experiences of a life-changing sort yet all but the most deprived of us experience human love and are blessed with a sense of natural beauty. To some of us this natural beauty and the joy that it evokes in us is a manifestation of the love for us of that power that has made us.

> *That light whose smile kindles the Universe,*
> *That Beauty in which all things work and move.*
> quoted in The Religion of Man.
> Rabindranath Tagore (45b)

As I write these words the flowers in the garden outside my window are in full bloom. Each flower is a work of art and the artist is not content with having them all the same. The variation in size, shape, perfume and colour give one the impression that this is beauty for beauty's sake. Nature is inviting us to recognise her creative genius and we are happy to do so for it lifts our spirits when we realise that we too are a part of nature's creation. It is not difficult to understand why Spinoza revered nature to the point where Nature and God were one.

If nature moves us by her beauty she also evokes in us a profound sense of wonder. I have already quoted Einstein and Poincaré on this theme and all those of us who have not lost our childhood sense of wonder and excitement of the world around us must share their response. Even if we accept that nothing exists that is not within our consciousness, that the Universe and all that is in it is essentially mental, yet we have to admit that of which we are conscious exceeds immeasurably our own capacity to conceive what we experience. Our sense of awe engendered by the study of nature is in part a realisation of this inequality between what we perceive and what we can conceive.

The effect that this realisation has is twofold. First, it induces a profound sense of reverence. Whatever the origin of the Universe and all it contains, it completely overwhelms our capacity to apprehend it. This inadequacy does not, however, induce a feeling in me that we are irrelevant in the scheme of things. However small we may be, we are not trivial and without even the least of us the Universe would not be complete. Science has revealed some of the properties of matter that make life possible and the power of nature to use those properties so creatively strikes all but the most ardent atheist, as both beautiful and ingenious.

I illustrate what I mean by a simple example. One of man's major achievements was the invention of the wheel. In the few thousand years since this intellectual triumph the wheel has become an essential part of a multitude of human activities. Why then did not nature make use of the wheel? My first attempt to answer this question was based on the realisation that there would be major technological problems in supplying a living rotating wheel with the nutrients essential to its maintenance. However, there is no such problem if the rotor is just one single molecule and indeed nature has produced such a rotor. This rotor is driven by chemical energy and serves to pump ions against an electro-chemical gradient. Were this mono-molecular rotor to stop all plant and animal life would die. The development of this device predates man's invention of the wheel by several billion years.

Were I to leave a discussion of the human condition at this point I would have to admit to being grossly dishonest. I started this book by expressing the need we have to comprehend not only those experiences in life that give us joy but also those that cause us grief. First, we may ask ourselves whether misfortune is just bad luck. If this were so we might live fearfully and even put our trust in lucky charms if we are pagan or in prayers of petition if we are religious. I cannot believe in a God that can create such a wondrous and beautiful Universe but who requires us to petition Him to spare us suffering. It seems to me that to hold such a belief is sacrilegious, it casts doubt on His wisdom and compassion. When my son was diagnosed with leukaemia certainly I prayed and since he died nevertheless, it may be said that my prayers were not answered. I now interpret that apparent failure in a very different way. I am sure that his death was meant to be and that he willingly chose what he came to us to do. In saying this of course I reveal that I do not believe that our life starts when we are born and finishes when we die. All that I have written in this book flies against such a supposition.

Death is certain for the born. Rebirth is certain for the dead. You should not grieve for what is unavoidable. Before birth, beings are not manifest to our human senses. In the interim between birth and death, they are manifest. At death they return to the unmanifest again. What is there in all this to grieve over?

Bhagavad-Gita (22b)

If, as Hinduism and Buddhism maintain we do pass through a cycle of birth, death and rebirth then we become ageless and even if we are largely ignorant of our true nature, yet there is the potential and the opportunity to make progress. The maturity with which my son went through his disease was far greater than one might expect of a young child, but if we are essentially timeless then he was incalculably older than his three years. Had he not died I might have been content to see only what the eye can see. It is true that I have been most fortunate in having parents who have shown me that the world of appearances provides a very incomplete view of what there is, but had it not been for the death of my son I do not believe that I would have felt the same need to explore as far as I could those things that are eternal. Now, when I recall the joy he gave us when he was here I still feel joy.

The reader may respond to this reasoning by pointing out that, whereas my son's death may have benefited me and others who knew him such a benefit was dearly bought by my son. However, if he is the mature, spiritual and loving being that I believe him to be and if, as I believe that the life after death, at least for those who have tried to live this life according to their light, is joyful and inspiring, then my son's death was his entry into this blessed state. As I believe the mystical feeling of love that I had as he was dying also embraced him, then he is secure and nurtured in a state of bliss. Those undergoing Near Death Experiences express just such an image of life after death; indeed, in some cases they are unwilling

121

to return to this life when told that they must. The comedian Michael Bentine put it well when he described death as passage through a door called 'Summer'.

It is in these terms that we should view all apparent disasters. We all recall the event of Boxing Day 2004 when an earthquake beneath the Indian Ocean generated a tidal wave that killed a quarter of a million people. The province of Aceh in Indonesia was most severely affected where some individuals lost all their living relations. Amazingly, a woman survivor, I think a Muslim, remarked afterwards 'God did not send the Tsunami to punish us but to teach us.' Such a courageous assertion requires us to enquire of ourselves just what we may learn. I think that there are several points on which to reflect. First, the death toll from the earthquake was no more than the number of people who die every day of every year. If we insist on death being the end of life then all life is tragic. It is evident that I do not accept this soul-crushing view. However, we are equally in error if we dismiss this life as being of little value. It is in dealing with the difficulties and vagaries of life that we develop our own compassion for others and grow spiritually ourselves. We need to remember that a child dies every 3 seconds in the poorer parts of the world – equivalent to a Tsunami every ten days. These deaths are avoidable. They are a challenge to our compassion. When we realise that the rich nations of the world spend some $50,000 on defence for each avoidable child death we realise just how geographically distorted is our evaluation of human life.

The Final State

If the reason for our being is to evolve spiritually we are naturally inclined to ask what should be the culmination of this development. All the great religions teach that ultimate perfection is attainable although a knowledge of in just what form that perfection resides is not accessible to us. Christ's exhortation to 'be perfect even as your Father in heaven is perfect' expresses the Christian belief in this final state of humankind, but if we recognise that God is ineffable and transcendental we cannot conceive of what this state of perfection may be.

Hinduism and Buddhism express our final destiny somewhat differently. For the Hindu we ultimately lose the illusion that we have carried with us so long, that we have a 'self' that is independent and separated from the real 'Self' which is Parabrahman.

At death he is born again, and the circumstances of his new life are determined by his past deeds and by the habits he has formed. He continues to live in the three states of consciousness – waking, dreaming, and dreamless sleep. As long as he continues in these states, he is the individual self. He as the Self, is infinite, indivisible; he is consciousness, bliss. In him are merged all three states of consciousness. From him are born mind, life, and the senses; earth, air, water, fire and ether. He is the reality behind all existence.

He is the Supreme Brahman. He is in all, he is the foundation of all. Subtler than the subtlest is he. He is eternal. Thou art he! Thou art he!   Kaivalya. The Upanishads. (40b)

George Fox, the 17 century mystic and founder of Quakerism maintained that there was that of God in everyone(52). If our spiritual development enables us to cast off those features of our individuality that serve to conceal this truth then there is nothing left but that of God in us. Thus the mysticism of this Christian mystic is not so distant from that of the Hinduism that was born in India several centuries before the birth of Christ.

For the Buddhist the final state, achieved after one escapes from samsara, the cycle of birth, death and rebirth, is one of enlightenment. Those who have not yet reached this stage lack the spiritual insight and resources to experience what it is. Thus Buddhism recognises the achievability of an ultimate goal but does not attempt to describe it. Given our total incomprehension of something as familiar to us as our own consciousness Buddha's recognition of our limitations is surely no more than one should expect.

The Hindu belief that 'Thou art he' is also expressed in a beautiful poem of one of the Sufi mystics. The poet also alludes to what the Buddhist might recognise as Nirvana.

The Vision of God in Everything

In the market, in the cloister – only God I saw,
In the valley and on the mountain – only God I saw,
Him I have seen beside me oft in tribulation;
In favour and in fortune – only God I saw.
In prayer and fasting, in praise and contemplation,

In the religion of the Prophet – only God I saw.
Neither soul nor body, accident nor substance,
Qualities nor causes – only God I saw.
I op'ed mine eyes and by the light of His face around me
In all the eye discovered – only God I saw.
Like a candle I was melted with His fire;
Amidst the flames outflanking – only God I saw.
Myself with mine own eyes I saw most clearly,
But when I looked with God's eyes – only God I saw.
I passed away into nothingness, I vanished,
And lo, I was the All-living – only God I saw.

Baba Kubi of Shiraz,
Translated by Nicholson, R.A. (19b)

Bibliography

1. Eddington, A.S. The Nature of the Physical World. Cambridge. 1928. Cited in ref. 5(c) below.
2. Ellison, A. The Paranormal: a Scientific Exploration of the Supernatural. Dodd Mead. New York. 1988. (a) p 23, p 43, (b) p 10, (c) p 7, (d) p 47-8
3. Myers, F.W.H. Human Personality and its Survival of Bodily Death. Published in two volumes in 1903 and reprinted in abridged form by Pelegrin Trust is association with Pilgrim Books. Norwich, England. (a) p 110-114, (b) Chapter VI, (c) p 247-8, (d) p 241-5
4. Dirac, P. The Evolution of the Physicists' Picture of Nature. Scientific American 208, 1963. p 45-53
5. Dampier, W.C. A History of Science and its relations with philosophy and religion. Cambridge University Press, 4th Edition. 1979. (a) p 1-200, (b) p 495, (c) cited on p 497, (e) cited on p174, (f) cited on p 197.
6. See for example, Brown, H. The Wisdom of Science: its relevance to Culture and Religion. Cambridge University Press. 1986. (a) p 74, (b) p 77, (c) p 82, (d).p 83, (e) p 86-90.
7. Barrow J.D., Tippler, F. J. The Anthropic Cosmological Principle. OUP 1988. (a) p 476, (b) p 77, (c) p 44, (d) p 147, (e) 524-541 (f) 250 (g) 143
8. Carr, B.J., Rees, M.J. The anthropic principle and the structure of the physical world. Nature 278 1979. p 605-612
9. cited in Magee, B. The Great Philosophers. BBC books 1987. p 129
10. Planck, M.
11. Tagore, R. Sãdhana. Macmillan & Co., Ltd. London. 1913. p 97
12. Weinberg, S. Nature 330 1987 pp 433-37. cited in Alexander, D. Rebuilding the Matrix. Lion Books. 2002. p 249

13. In-Outline of Modern Belief. Eds. Sullivan, J.W.N., and W. Grierson. George Newnes Ltd. (a) p 510, (b) p 878 (c) p 523, (d) p 786, (e) p 520, (f) p 520

14. Bender, H. Poltergeists. In-Psychical Research. A Guide to its History, Principles and Practices. In celebration of 100 years of the Society for Psychical Research. Ed. Grattan-Guiness, I. Aquarian Press. 1982.

15. Fontana, D. Is there an afterlife? O Books, 2005 p64-76

16. Gauld, A., A.D. Cornell. Poltergeists. Routledge & Kegan Paul. 1979.

17. Chalmers, D.J. Facing up to the Problem of Consciousness. J. Consciousness Studies. 2: 1995. p 200-219

18. James, W. The Varieties of Religious Experience. Longmans, Green & Co. USA. 1902. Reprinted in Penguin Classics. 1985. (a) p 490, (b) p 394, (c) p 498

19. Happold, F.C. Mysticism: a Study and an Anthology. Penguin Books. England 1st Edition 1963, reprinted 1981. (a) p 39, (b) p 251

20. In-Radin, D. The Conscious Universe. The scientific truth of psychic phenomena. Harper, San Francisco. 1997. (a) cited on p 111, (b) p 88, (c) cited on p 91, (d) p 91-191, (e) p 98 105, (f) cited on p 96-97

21. Guerney, E., F.W.H. Myers, F. Podmore. Phantasms of the Living. Published in 1886 and republished in 1970 in Scholars' Facsimiles & Reprints. Gainsville, Florida.

22. Bhagavad-Gita. The Song of God. Trans. Swami Prabhavanda and C.I. Isherwood. Dent. London. 1975. (a) p 28, (b) p 43

23. Swami Prabhavanda. The Spiritual Heritage of India. Sri Ramakrishna Math. Madras. 1977. (a) p 165, (b) p 70, (c) p 351

24. Wilson, I. The After Death Experience. Sigwick & Jackson. London. 1987. (a) p 54-7, (b) p 46

25. Psychical Research. A Guide to its History, Principles and Practices. In celebration of 100 years of the Society for Psychical Research. Ed. Grattan-Guiness, I. Aquarian Press. 1982.

26. Sinclair, U. Mental Radio. Werner Laurie. London. 1930.

27. Ducasse, C.J. A Critical Examination of the Belief in a Life after Death. Springfield, Ill. Charles C. Thomas. 1961.

28. Wilson, I. Mind Out of Time? Victor Gollancz Ltd. London. 1981.

29. Driesch, H. Psychical Research. The Science of the Supernormal. G. Bell & Sons Ltd. London. 1933. (a) p 157, (b) p 157

30. James, W. The Psychological Review. July. 1898. p 421-22.

31. Hardy, A. The Divine Flame. First published by Collins, London & Glasgow 1966. Reproduced by RERU by permission of the publishers. 1978. Cited on p 178

32. Perry, M. Psychic Studies. A Christian View. Aquarian Press. Northamptonshire. 1984. (a) p 30, (b) p 9, (c) p183

33. Hick, J. The Fifth Dimension. One World. Oxford. 1999. p 242

34. Fisher, J. The Case for Reincarnation. Grafton Books. London. 1986. (a) Cited on p 99, (b) p 77-8

35. Plato. Phaedo. The Death of Socrates. Doubleday. New York. NY. 1973. p 505.

36. Ducasse, C.J. How the case of *The Search for Bridey Murphy* stands today. J. Amer. Soc. Psychical Res. 54. 1960. p 3-22.

37. Becker, C.B. Paranormal Experience and Survival of Death. SUNY Press. 1993. (a) p 18, (b) p 25-33

38. Stevenson, I. The Evidence for Survival from Claimed Memories of former Incarnations. J. Amer. So. Psychical Res. Vol.54. 1958.

39. Stevenson, I. MD. Twenty Cases Suggestive of reincarnation. Univ. Press of Virginia. 2nd Edition. 1974.

40. The Upanishads. translated by Swami Prabhavananda and F. Manchester. Mentor Religious Classics. New York. 1960. (a) p 109, (b) p 115

41. Roy, A.E. Precognition-a Sort of Radar. In- Psychical Research. A Guide to its History, Principles and Practices. In celebration of 100 years of the Society for Psychical Research. Ed. Grattan-Guiness, I. Aquarian Press. 1982. Chapter 10.

42. Barker, J.C. Premonitions of the Aberfan Disaster. J. Soc. Psychical Res. 44, 1967. p 169-181

43. Rhine, J. B. The Reach of the Mind. Faber & Faber. London. 1948.

44. Schmidt, H. Precognition of a quantum process. J. Parapsychology. 33, 1969.

45. Tagore, R. The Religion of Man. Unwin Books. London. 4th impression. 1970. (a) p 123, (b) p.64

46. Robinson, E. Ed. Living the Questions. The Religious Experience Research Unit. Manchester College. Oxford. (a)p 126, (b)p 104

47. From: Quaker Faith and Practice. The Yearly Meeting of the Religious Society of Friends (Quakers) in Britain.1995. (a) 26.08, (b) 21.27, (c) 19.32

48. Jones, R. New Studies in Mystical Religion. Macmillan & Co Ltd. London. 1927.

49. Moody, R. Life after Life. Rider, London. 2001.

50. Fenwick, P., E. Fenwick. The truth in the light. London. Hodder Headline. 1995.

51. Ring, K. Mindsight: Eyeless Vision in the Blind. In-Thinking Beyond the Brain. Ed. Lorimer, D. Floris Books. 2001. p 59-70

52. In the letter of George Fox from Launceton prison in 1656. Cited in 47 (c)